< A C0 BFB 554 A >

Trade-Offs

FOR THE PERSON WHO CAN'T HAVE EVERYTHING

David Hon

LEARNING CONCEPTS

Jacket design by Suzanne Pustejovsky
Book design and production by Mary Ann Noretto
Illustrations by Suzanne Pustejovsky and Mike Krone
Composition by Gary Nored

Trade-Offs
ISBN 0-89384-048-3
Library of Congress Catalogue No. 80-39625

©1981 by David Hon.

First Printing January 1981

Learning Concepts
Austin, Texas

Distributed by
University Associates
8517 Production Avenue
P.O. Box 26240
San Diego, California 92126

*To my
wife,
Brenda*

CONTENTS

Why Trade-Offs?

Because we talk daily, even hourly, about them. We *think* about them much more. And we call them trade-offs as easily and fluently as we use any term in business language. That alone makes it clear that we know we *are* traders.

But is trading off taught in schools? Is trading a required course for an MBA? Any manager will say it is a superior ability, but just where is this skill of balancing trade-offs being learned?

In the streets. On the drawing boards. At the conference table. Any place that real experience is gained, we see students of trade-offs. Because you've been there, you'll realize that this book attempts—in a speculative way—to put those real-life trade-offs in perspective. If you haven't been there, *Trade-Offs* may orient you in this "savvy" that separates an experienced manager from a new one, a good trader from an average one.

Some will say *Trade-Offs* is a book about power, and others will say it is a decision-making book. But it is neither. Trade-offs govern your position when power is brought to bear and decisions must be made. Trade-offs come *before* decisions are made (as well as during and after), and their many lives are what this book will explore.

1

The Everyday World

---

*trade-off n. 1. a balancing of factors all of
which are not attainable at the
same time 2. a giving up of one
thing in return for another.*

Webster's New Collegiate Dictionary, 1976

The term *trade-off* has only recently gained the respectability
of a dictionary entry. It has lived a shadowy life as a colloquial term used by executives, politicians, generals, and other
decision makers who do indeed have to *balance* factors "all of
which are not attainable" in a particular situation. Just because
the term isn't in our everyday vocabulary doesn't mean that all
of us have not weighed factors daily for our own trade-offs. We
do. We must. We always have.

Trade-offs are our attempt to strike an equilibrium in judgement. Most often this balance is created and maintained as a set of relative "importances" which we form before any decision making takes place. So trade-offs represent a *predecision-making posture* that provides a key to all decisions which follow.

Everyday trade-offs encompass a broad range of concerns, but a balanced trade-off always seems to consider *quality, cost,* and *time.* Whether the trade-offs are simple or complex, they inevitably balance these three elements. Moreover, the people who balance trade-offs well are the mysteriously successful among us.

These people seem to carry three finely honed tools—their concepts of *quality, cost,* and *time*—into every situation to make trades that will work well for them in the future. They are full-time traders. They know that they are always on a trading ground—one as well defined in their minds as a market place for caravans. To some extent we are all traders. Having tools well-sharpened and knowing where the best trades are is quite another matter.

We negotiate most trade-offs without realizing what we are doing. They seem to arise naturally and, like the sticker price of an automobile, our trade-off patterns seem fixed. But trade-offs vary dramatically, and we may well observe that most conflicts and misunderstandings come from disharmonious trade-off patterns.

Here's one example:

A certain cinematographer makes high quality film for movies and takes pride in his superior craftsmanship. He climbs mountains, hangs from moving vehicles, and lies on his stomach in the mud—anything to get first-rate footage.

Between movie jobs this cinematographer joins The Six O'Clock News as a remote cameraman and finds that his concern for quality puts him at a distinct disadvantage. The news business requires quick filming and low cost; the quality of the shots is secondary. One day he spends four hours at the city park pie-eating contest, getting wonderful shots of the merriment. Seven reels of pie eating. Surprise! He is fired by the Six O'Clock News director.

"But this is great footage," he says.

"We need shots of the six-car pile-up and the opening of the new Japanese Garden," says the news director.

"I was just trying to get high quality stuff on the news," says the cinematographer. "What's the world coming to, when you get fired for producing quality?"

WHAT IS IT COMING TO, INDEED?

The cinematographer and the Six O'Clock News director had different sets of trade-offs. The cinematographer chose high quality—whatever the cost and time.

The news director, after all, had to produce The Six O'Clock News . . . every night of the year. He had once been a cinematographer, and when he joined a news team, he began trading off quality because it cost too much and took too long. Having to fire someone because he produced quality footage was a tough decision. What, he anguished, is the world coming to?

The world is where it always was . . . cost, quality, and time are there to be balanced, and what we do depends on the *relative importance* we have assigned to each one. If we decide that time is of the essence, we'll pay for it or accept minimum quality that does the job.

If low cost is most important, we'll trade off a lot of time looking, or we'll buy a dependable Chevy instead of a classy Cadillac.

If we decide, as did the cinematographer, that quality is the most important thing in life, we will pay and spend the time necessary to get it. The trick, then, is to have your trade-offs aligned according to what you're doing and whom you're doing it with.

Options

Let's consider the options of both news director and cinematographer. *The cinematographer* might have:

1. Done one or two takes, then called in for the next story. (However, he feels that this is professionally "wrong.")
2. Taken another job where the management values quality as much as he does (if he can find one . . .).
3. Reached a compromise with the news director, such as shooting one out of four stories at a ratio of four to one, but the rest at two to one.

The Six O'Clock News director could have:

1. Hired a cinematographer for "quick" takes and assigned this one to features (if he has a feature budget).
2. Allotted the cinematographer one roll of film per story (thereby saving cost but maybe not time if the takes are short ones).
3. Suggested that the cinematographer find another job where quality is valued (which is why he fired him).

One of these alternatives might have prevented their parting company. They might at least have reduced their surprise and agony if they had had a simple way of discussing and illustrating trade-off patterns—a triangle which shows the importance of each factor by the degrees of the angles. If all factors were given equal weight, an equilateral triangle could represent them.

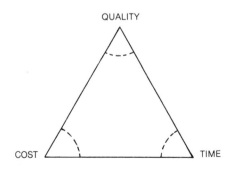

However, our trade-offs are usually not so equal. Imagine a company where there is an ongoing dispute between the marketing people who want to get a product out rapidly (time-oriented) and the finance people who don't want to pay over-time to speed up production (cost-oriented). Here's Marketing's triangle, with the widest angle representing high cost and a small angle representing their desire for low time.

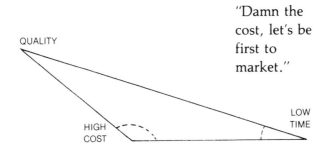

"Damn the cost, let's be first to market."

Here's Finance's triangle, with low cost shown by a small angle and high time with a wide angle.

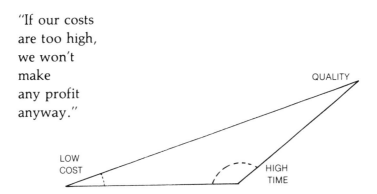

"If our costs are too high, we won't make any profit anyway."

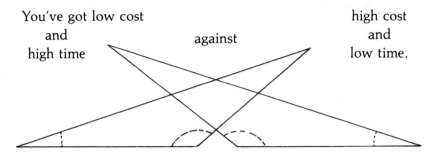

You've got low cost and high time   against   high cost and low time.

It looks like the twain will never meet. But the marketing people and the finance people have lunch together to scheme. They scrutinize inspectors in Manufacturing who send back many nearly perfect units. They raise their eyebrows at the fine grade of materials used in every facet of production, saying to themselves:

"Who needs that much quality?"

Twixtward One

One option for the marketing and the finance people would be to induce the manufacturing people to put some inspectors back on the production line and buy adequate but lower *cost* materials. In this way, both Marketing and Finance can get what they want.

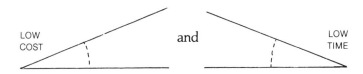

But carrying the logic of classical geometry out to the trade-off triangle, a large angle would seem to indicate that quality would be high,

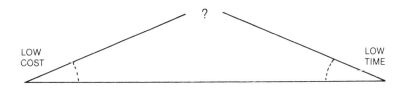

which of course we know it would not be. So, we'll abandon classical geometry in constructing triangles to illustrate our trade-offs and simply say:

The quality angle is different.

Quality is an ideal.

And we'll construct a quality angle to represent the amount we vary from the ideal.

This angle then represents high quality,

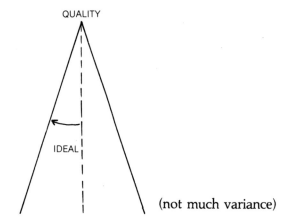

(not much variance)

while this one represents low quality.

(a lot of variance)

How we get our ideals of quality and how we then use them in our trade-offs will be the subject of the next chapter.

2

Quality

Our sense of quality forges random realities into useful dreams.

Quality is not always as subjective as we may have been taught to think. Seen in a pragmatic way, it can be defined and used by anyone. When elevated to the abstract and theoretical, it retains some mystery. It would help separate the workaday from the mysterious, if we looked at quality in a hierarchy.

Quality as Existence

The first step one encounters in judging quality, and later in trading it off, is questioning whether something exists at all. We have a hard time judging whether a roar and flash of lights is a superior or average flying saucer. First of all, let's decide whether or not it was a flying saucer. Usually, the existence of a thing is given when we consider quality. Sometimes, the thing isn't there at all.

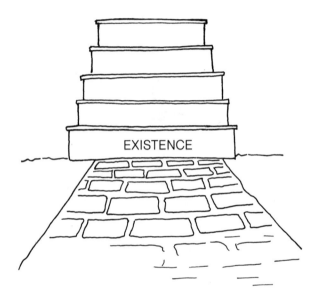

Until we know whether or not something exists, we cannot approach the first step of the quality hierarchy. This first rung seems to be common sense, although it often is not, especially when dealing with rumors and innuendoes. "Will Charlotte's break-up with her husband be detrimental to her kids?" is irrelevant until we know that Charlotte and Bob are really breaking up. Certainly it would be too early to judge how this will affect the kids' upbringing. Until we determine that a state or thing truly exists, we cannot begin to evaluate its quality.

Quality as Validity

Once we are fairly certain something exists, our next step in thinking about quality is to decide whether the thing is or isn't what it purports to be. A corollary is whether it works or not.

For years, Florida land dealers sold "beach-front property" that was swampland. Outraged buyers weren't concerned about the quality of swamp they had. They knew they had land, but this was damned poor beach front.

We really can't judge the quality of a child's 69-cent "watch" that has hands fixed at eight o'clock, because it doesn't work like a watch is supposed to. It doesn't even fit a common definition of "watch"; it exists but is not a *valid* watch.

There are a lot of things that aren't what they purport to be or don't work like they're supposed to. There are many marriages that aren't marriages, businesses that are operated as money-losers for holding companies, dwellings that invite rain and rats and are used only as tax shelters. It's enough to say that we cannot judge or trade off the quality of something until we're reasonably sure that it is what it purports to be.

Quality as Tolerance

Tolerance is some leeway allowed for variation from a standard. Anyone who has manufactured anything in volume is familiar with the concept of *tolerance.* A bag of cookies has 16 ounces of cookies *plus or minus* one ounce. New lawn furniture may have to be beaten with a hammer when it is assembled so that ill-shaped parts fit together. You may even have to drill new holes, because the original ones were manufactured with a wide tolerance. Each piece may not be exactly like another off the production line because:

1. The manufacturing system was not designed to produce close consistency.
2. Quality control was lax or nonexistent.

In manufacturing, production time and cost rise as tolerance levels become closer. It is much more expensive to manufacture a product that will not vary more than one one-thousandth inch than to produce one that will vary no more than one one-hundredth inch.

Closer tolerances must be closer to *something,* and even the first expression of some ideal can be the basis for a useful standard. Semanticists call the language of ideals and standards *directive language.* The ideal is stated, but not expected to be achieved. "A scout is cheerful," one of twelve rules of scouting, is not a statement of fact. It states a condition scouts would *like* to exist. This statement provides a direction or ideal standard of performance as a scout. "The ideal bag of cookies *will have* sixteen ounces of pure cookie" is an awfully demanding expectation in producing a million boxes. But it forms a useful standard against which to work when you add a statement of expected variance, "within 5 percent either way, of course."

Sometimes the standard is set arbitrarily—16 ounces of pure cookie ±5 percent—just so we *will* have a standard to work against. Other times we use an average to establish the standard, but you don't have to get embroiled in statistical means and standard deviations to do this.

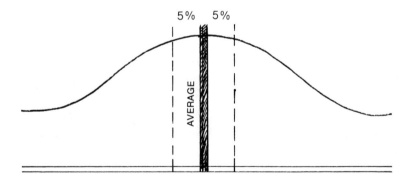

Say we are talking about the weight for men who are 5 feet 10 inches, age thirty-five. Their average weight may be 160 pounds, and we could declare that plus or minus 10 percent falls within the range of "normal" (especially for those of us tipping the scale at 175). In this case, an "average" determined our ideal, and we arbitrarily set the variance we wanted for our standard.

Sometimes ideals interlock, like the many parts of automobiles. The ideal car never develops piston slap because the piston fits exactly into the cylinder and the rings seat perfectly for the first 500 miles. Your car and mine may not have been tooled exactly to this ideal standard. A 5 percent tolerance in manufacturing the piston plus a 5 percent tolerance in manufacturing the cylinder could allow a 10 percent variance overall. That piston rattling in the cylinder could send us to the shop for a 20,000-mile engine overhaul.

The concept of tolerance is crucial to constructing and using the trade-off triangle introduced in the first chapter. If you use small angles to illustrate low cost and low time, you end up with a wide angle that means *low* quality. If you trade off cost or time or both and increase those angles, you get a small angle that means high quality. What we see in our two quality angles is the amount of *variance* from the ideal that we would accept.

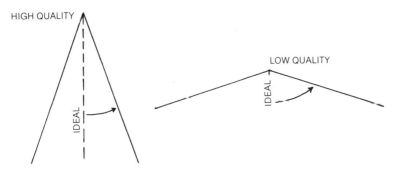

This perception of quality has been useful to science and industry and could be extremely useful to all walks of life. To know that a scout is not always cheerful—that cheerfulness is only an ideal—is the first step toward making quality trade-offs. We must make them always, or we will go mad in a world that does not allow us to achieve the ideal. People who operate with an affinity for close tolerances assure themselves and the world of the highest possible quality in whatever they produce. People who condone a wider tolerance on occasion probably do so because they are trading *some* quality for reduced time or cost. They can never trade off *all* quality; the product would not be what it purports (losing validity) and may not even survive at all (losing existence).

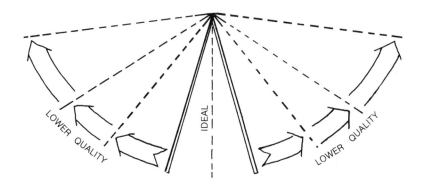

Quality as Fantasy Bank

On the other hand, we arrive at another concept of quality through an accumulated perception of *what is missing*, a process logicians might call *negative induction*. We begin with the words *if only*.

> *"If only* that long ball hadn't been foul"
> *"If only* the bases had been loaded when the homer was hit"
> *"If only* we'd been in the last of the ninth inning when the grand slam was hit"
> *"If only* it'd been the deciding game of the World Series when the grand slam homer was hit in the last of the ninth"

Do you see how we accumulate "if only's" in our fantasy banks? Here are some more.

"If only he were rich as well as handsome"
"If only the price of steel were lower"
"If only someone could love the real me"
"If only the trucking service offered more dependable delivery"
"If only there weren't such high tariffs on imported woolen goods"
"If only the supermarket would have a sale on avocados before my dinner party"
"If only I lived closer to work"
"If only I had an MBA"

The reason "if only's" come so easily to mind is that we have so many in our fantasy banks. Each concept of some ideal, from the perfect World Series game ending to the perfect mate, has a special deposit box in the fantasy bank. By the time we have much *experience* with a concept, our fantasy bank is full. Perhaps that is what experience gives us more than anything else: a more highly refined perception of an ideal.

When we have a full fantasy bank, we can better judge when circumstances are best for action.

> "He's rich and *fairly* good looking. Guess I'll marry him."
> "The price of steel is still going up but more slowly than before. Now is the time to build a supply for those cable orders we get in the winter."
> "Tariffs on woolens are being cut in half. Let's move from 100 percent polyester to a blend in our fall line."

Let's go back to the perception of ideal quality that our fantasy bank affords. We derive our ideals and standards of perfection from that perception, both as individuals and as generations. These ideals all come from amassing "if only's." And the combination of our "if only's" determines our usual ideal of quality—a combination of attributes, things, and circumstances that we would like to exist but that rarely does.

Quality as Intuition

Our concepts of quality based on an average, a necessary standard, or a process of negative induction are fairly easy to understand. It is less easy for us to fathom our awareness of quality in our intuition. We *do* have intuitions about quality that are more often correct than deceived.

This awareness is like our sensory understanding of the slam of a car door. The door's sound and weight and the pressure we exert on the handle all contribute to our understanding of its secure closing. We can tell one slam from another and know a particular door's quirks, without even knowing what stimuli we are taking in and processing.

It is astounding how our intuitions are very often right about quality. We process information naturally—half consciously—as we do when slamming a car door. Perhaps we have an internal handicapper sizing up the odds . . . .

You know how handicappers work at the track. They assess the horse's past performance, breeding, temperament, and then make the leap of the hunch on how the jockey, track conditions, and every other nuance of that particular race will interact—and come out with the odds. They make their living by those odds not getting beaten by too much too often.

Deep inside us, we have an oddsmaker that processes millions of stimuli a day we're not conscious of. That's the slam of the car door we take for granted, the conclusion we reach faster and more accurately than any high-speed computer.

That oddsmaker is called "intuition." When we free intuition to call our bets, unencumbered by our conscious mind, it is surprisingly successful.

Timothy Gallwey's book *The Inner Game of Tennis* calls intuition the best playing mechanism for sports. And how many "gut feelings" in business really determine the outcome of a project? There may be more wisdom than self-indulgence in playing life this way.

Yet the battle in one's mind is always on, between the oddsmaker's hunch that "it feels right" and the analysis that says "it

figures." These two phrases aren't formed in our language acci-
dentally. Although colloquial, they are more apt than even
psycholinguists might suspect, because:

They represent our minds groping

and bartering for top quality.

Robert Ornstein and other brain researchers now say that
our analytical processes ("it figures") occur in the left side of the
brain and that our intuitive processes ("it feels right") occur in
the right. Before the results are in about where these processes
are housed, we do know that we engage in both analytical and
intuitive "thought." Most of us experience some conflict between those analytical and intuitive thought processes, and
from that conflict the brute question on your management style
emerges: How much do you trust your logic, your pocket
calculator, and your computer compared to that twinge in your
insides—how much do you trust your handicapper?

In the hierarchy of quality, the lower realms are quite logical
and pragmatic, but as quality rises toward higher levels of
abstraction, our perceptions appear less rational and more subjective.

When approaching steeper grades of quality, the air seems
rarefied. That's when perceptions of quality become internalized. First, those groups of people with intense experience and
special expertise in their fields may have a highly developed
sense of quality in their fantasy banks. Bookbinders may, for
example, have a highly developed fantasy bank on bookbind-
ing—with lofty ideals about the perfect binding. Their ideals
may exceed those of librarians, for instance. But, this refined
perception of quality is what signals their expertise. Being in
agreement with the perceptions of other experts is often a
measure of sensitive recognition of quality.

With intuition, the process of perceiving quality may be
internalized for each individual, but the validity of that percep-

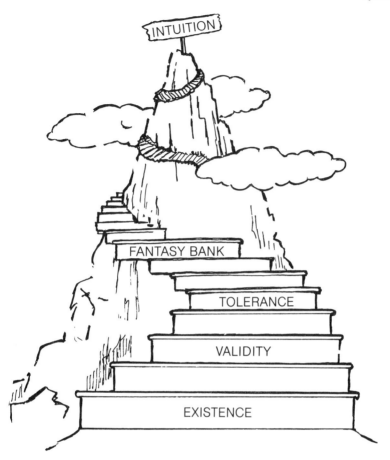

tion can usually be tested against the fantasy banks of some expert groups. Individual intuitions about quality cannot exist in a vacuum and be useful and effective; they must eventually fit somebody's fantasy bank to be accepted.

What's intriguing, of course, is the notion that individual intuition occasionally discovers an ideal of quality that is at once universal and was previously unperceived even in the other experts' fantasy banks. This accounts for historic "great leaps," like Einstein's, and for our individual triumphs when we acted on a "gut feeling."

Two Common Quality Trade-Offs

The two most easily observed qualities we deal with daily are "quality of product" and "quality of life." Our perceptions of those are formed at some level of the quality hierarchy.

Quality of product involves envisioning the quality of something one presents to the world. Because it is communication of one's own self to the world, it cannot be—and is not—taken lightly by most people. That's what makes quality trade-offs in business so difficult.

Both quality of life and quality of product reflect how things would ideally be, *if only* . . . .

One might choose a job that allows many hours at home or one that demands extensive entertaining. In either case, the *quality* involved in the trade-off is quality of life. Many who sought fame discovered that they traded off privacy and anonymity and had to reexamine what quality of life meant, just as we all have to decide what the quality angle in our trade-offs means to us.

Twixtward Two

If you see that quality can be represented as the degree of departure from an ideal, you may easily derive a triangle which trades off more time and cost for higher quality.

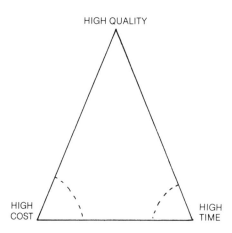

Or lower quality for less time and cost.

The size of an angle represents how *important* that element is to you. So, as you might imagine, there are infinite variations in importance we can give each angle of the triangle. But to get a better hold on all three elements, let us examine cost and time in a bit more detail. These two factors, along with quality, are what we traders must see clearly in each trade-off situation we enter.

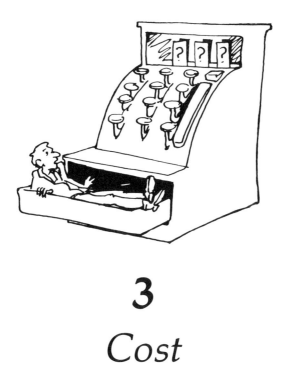

3

Cost

The cost of anything can vary between nothing and your life.

Two regular features of evening newscasts are reports on the weather and the stock market. Both are always "news"— partly because they are never completely predictable and partly because we have the lingering belief that what happens today will help us predict the future.

The weather forecast and stock market closings are similar in another way that gets us to the crux of cost. Just as the weather depends on natural currents, so does the worth of any stock and its resulting cost. Just as the weather report ventures nightly to *predict* that the flow of a cold air mass beneath a hot humid one means snow, the cost of a given stock (or an indicator for the whole market) is a predictor of the flow of worth in business affairs. If a stock closes ten points higher than it did yesterday, it means that investors think this company will make them more money than it did before. If it falls ten points, investors predict the stock won't make them as much money.

Cost as a Balance Point

When the weather forecasters predict snow, they see the factors indicating snow near a balance point. Before that point, there will be no snow and just after it, snow will fall.

Cost—of a stock or a new refrigerator—behaves in the same way: it finds a *balance point,* up to which the seller doesn't want to sell and after which the buyer doesn't want to buy. This is only one of our perceptions of cost: that point at which the seller sells and the buyer buys.

Cost as Potential Difference

On either side of that balance point we're calling cost is the difference it will make if (1) the item is not sold or (2) the item is sold. In weather, of course, there is tremendous potential difference if hurricane winds are mounting and little potential difference if one lazy high pressure zone is moving toward another. Knowledge of high and low pressure zones allows meteorologists to forecast both wind velocity and direction several hours in advance. They observe conditions at a *balance point* and forecast a *flow* due to the unequal nature of high and low pressure areas. The science of electricity places more stress on the potential difference a flow can make. The measurement of electrical charge, voltage, is based on what *would* happen if current were applied.

Wants and needs, money and goods and services are a flow also, always from supply to demand, like electrons seeking atomic equilibrium after having been stirred up. Cost is a measurement—taken at the *balance point* before the flow of a transaction. If you spend money, one thing is likely to happen (or not happen), and if you don't spend it, another thing is likely to happen (or not happen).

---

1. Cost is a *balance point.*

2. The amount of cost is a measure-ment of *potential difference.*

If you see cost as a measure of potential difference, you can also see cost as . . .

Protection and Investment

We often buy protection *against* what could happen. That is *cost.* We also buy *into* something that will happen. That too is cost. Those are the only two reasons we spend money or trade away anything else we have to pay with (shells, diamonds, land, etc.).

That should be repeated. The only two things we pay for are

protection

and

investment.

Obviously, protection is reactive and investment is pro-active. But often a good investment is also protection against some future occurrence, say, inflation. (The best defense is a good offense.) The really important thing here is that our perception of cost as protection and investment comes from our perception of the *potential difference* it could make. We spend, we evaluate the cost by the potential difference we see between the future and the status quo. The measure of cost is the measure of its potential difference at the balance point between flows.

We perceive a cost to *be* that balance point. It is like turning current in an electrical wire on or off. At that balance point we decide that a thing happens or doesn't happen. Then we get sophisticated and decide *how much* we want to happen or not happen.

We all pay for protection to the extent that we see the future as more damaging than the status quo. We all invest in making the future better than the status quo.

When you sit at the balance point between now and the future, the investment–protection distinctions begin to blur. When you pay your telephone bill, you not only invest in the ability to communicate rapidly world-wide but protect yourself against having your phone taken out. In the business world, the ability to have and to communicate information turns the investment in complex inventory and order entry systems into necessities, which become a form of protection in rapidly changing competitive situations.

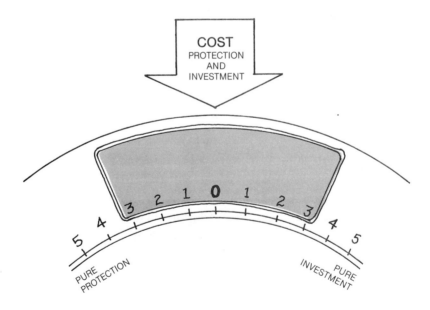

Pure protection can be bought in the form of term insurance from any agent. A pure investment is hard to find. A college education was seen at one time as an investment, a running start into professions, big money, and all that. The supply of college grads filled the demand, and this investment is now considered necessary for belonging. Buying membership in a middle class society is really just buying protection now. (The reversing economic situations of white- and blue-collar workers may soon bring that whole premise into question.) Perhaps the only pure investments are wagers, where the value of the investment is determined solely in terms of risking everything for a payoff. If the outcome is not secure, then there is no element of protection.

Worth in Context

Cost is an individual perception of worth: what the future will hold in terms of protection and investment. The duration and breadth of these perceptions creates what may be called a "worth context." And worth contexts change.

A worth context may be easily seen in foreign exchange rates for the dollar. The dollar rises and falls in comparison to other currencies. What is being predicted here is not just the success or failure of a company, but of a nation. The way the United States conducts itself, how productive it is, how much energy it has to buy, whether it is at war, and numerous very *subjective* variables are used by currency traders to decide how many deutschemarks they should exchange for one dollar. Those things make up the worth context of the dollar from day to day, even minute to minute.

Other examples?

The store where an item is sold—at Neiman-Marcus the same item may cost twice as much as it does in other stores because of the worth context.

The location of property—the same house may cost two or three times as much in a fashionable area as in a less fashionable one.

The special atmosphere of a restaurant can quadruple prices for the same entrée served down the street.

Brand names may be 50 percent higher than store brands because packaging and advertising create a worth context for the package contents.

The world doesn't need to be as high-priced as we sometimes make it. But it is often worth it to us psychologically to buy at the higher cost. We pay for mental well-being rather than physical well-being. (A current research study shows that a higher percentage of low income families buy higher priced brand-name products than do the middle or higher income families. In that small way, they are buying small parcels of psychological well-being, maybe in the form of protection against the unknown.)

Marketing—Finding Worth Contexts

Worth contexts are collective perceptions about the future just as protection and investment are individual perceptions about the future. The survival of any business, of course, depends upon its ability to operate within the prevailing worth contexts. And that's what marketing is all about—finding and defining worth contexts.

In the purest scheme of things, marketing should seek out or predict worth contexts *before* a product or service is developed to fit within that context. Often, however, a company will create a product with insufficient evidence that there *is* a worth context. Then they will send the marketing people out, product in hand, to *find* a worth context. Often they do. Often they don't. When they *do* score by finding a worth context, their company officials feel the marketing was good. That's incorrect. When they don't score, the officials feel the marketing was poor. That's right, but not in the way they suppose. What was really wrong was the design of the products for market, not the marketing of those products—desperately trying to find buyers.

"Finding a market" by advertising messages is not creative chicanery as popular wisdom goes; it really involves casting a large net to find a small worth context. We don't object to advertisements that tell us that something we've needed is now available. That's no ad, that's good news. What we dislike is being subjected to those ads that don't offer anything to fill *our* needs. What is happening, of course, is that the company marketeers are casting a large net for a worth context, hoping that somewhere out in prime time there is some segment of the population secretly yearning for a dog deodorant but knowing not where to turn.

Cost—Reflecting and Creating a Worth Context

When worth contexts are discovered, costs rise in anticipation, reflecting those contexts. But when people pay the costs, worth contexts are also expanded, or recreated in a cyclical fashion. Here are some good examples.

MODERN ART—Once an artist has an established style and has sold one painting for $2,000, then the rest of his paintings, even if they were done before the $2,000 sale and are lower quality, tend to cost more. Someone's paying that price actually created a worth context for all the paintings.

FUTURE OPTIONS—The wildest cost game in the world is buying future options in anything, especially agricultural commodities. True odds-making gamblers bet whether the worth context at a future date will make it profitable to exercise their options to buy. Sometimes these people are also in a position to withhold products from the market to increase costs and profits or to "dump" them on the market and decrease someone else's profits. Large holders sometimes threaten a dump so they can corner the market and then withhold the supply to raise prices.

The Balance Point . . . For How Long

As a measure of the potential difference between our present and future, cost represents a balance point of our personal universe. What we pay, and whether we pay, portends a flow in one direction or the other of all the natural and psychological forces that make up our existence. It's not that you must pay something to get something. Not at all. It's that *something* is going to happen regardless. With the costs you set and the costs you pay, you parcel out your being to stay in balance with the currents of your universe. Cost is your only measure of where that balance point is and what the potential difference is between now and the future. Worth contexts help define your costs, so a logical question would be:

How long does a worth context last?

Twixtward Three

If you are a manager of anything, a household or an international cartel, you are a trader. Good traders, of course, know all they can about quality and cost, two of the three "tools" with which traders pattern their trade-offs.

In a trade-off triangle, the quality angle represents the amount quality varies from an ideal. Higher quality would be shown by a narrow angle (or closer *tolerance*)

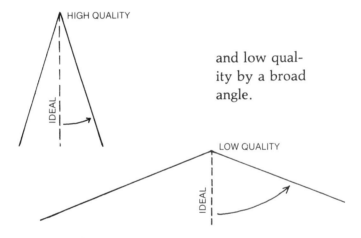

HIGH QUALITY

IDEAL

and low quality by a broad angle.

LOW QUALITY

IDEAL

On the other hand, the importance of cost in the trade-off triangle is directly proportional to the size of the angle.

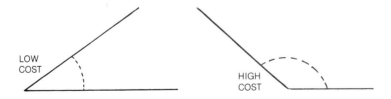

LOW COST

HIGH COST

Cost is the balance point of worth, the measure of potential difference between having something or not having it, of something happening or not happening. If you pay a high cost for something, it is usually to gain higher quality or possession more quickly.

The best traders know all this and know one more thing. They know about time. So it is the best traders who will ask:

"How long does a worth context last?"

4

Time

At the tone the time will be . . . too late.

There was an outer space comic book in which aliens put the hero through a cosmic rite of passage by placing him on a huge checkerboard floor. He had to make it to the edge while every few seconds they sent a high voltage electric shock into one or another configuration of squares, so he had to keep moving and not stay too long in one place.

Of all the metaphors for time (rivers, oceans, desert sands), this electric checkerboard seems most apropos. It's reminiscent of brave northerners who run across broken ice floes in early spring, skipping across ice slabs that would tilt or sink under someone's full weight, but are sturdy enough to *move across.* In the most dangerous mountain climbing, there are places on certain faces where you cannot find a handhold within reach. You must slide across a flat surface with the friction of the palm of your hand and a push off from a foothold below. Here as in the outer space comic (and on the ice floe) the essence of time—and survival—is rhythm. Time moves with us in perfect harmony if its rhythms are honored. However, if the climber freezes in mid-movement, the ice runner stops on a slab, or the hero hesitates on a single square, all is lost. The universe turns like a dog with a mean streak, going for the throat of the offender of time.

We need not get so dramatic. Try driving twenty on a freeway, or slow down in the fast lane to glance at a map. You can't. You must drive "in time" on a freeway.

Anyone in business knows about timing, not only about what products to order in March (for-delivery-by-July, to-be-stocked-by-October, to-sell-at-Christmas). But subtler things like, "How long can I go without paying vendors so that I can accrue an extra month's interest on something I've written off my income tax."

There is another kind of timing called "momentum." Momentum matches the velocity of our actions with the velocity of events. The phrase "bringing a new manager *up to speed*" is no casual metaphor. It recognizes that the endeavors of an organization *do* have a velocity, and the whole operation has a momentum in a single direction. That is why those who "drag their feet" are sometimes criticized.

The business world is exciting to many people because momentum can be a thrashing, headlong plunge that will not succeed if there are constant second thoughts or grinding slow-downs. In many situations allowing your momentum to be slowed, when closing a deal or getting out a product, is more than that violation of rhythm that will get you to the next handhold or ice slab. It represents a loss of faith, a dissipation of vital energy, a disregard of premises crucial to maintaining a worth context.

So time *is* the freeway, where you are always much better off jumping from one moving car to another than onto the road. Time can be seen as the velocity of events, through life, fortune, and successive orbits of human endeavor. Momentum, pacing, and timing—the many rhythms, sometimes syncopating, and sometimes leaving yearning silences—are singular expressions of our perceptions of time.

Let's see one reason why. Go back to the electrified checkerboard or the floating ice slabs. And recall the notion of *worth contexts* introduced in the last chapter. Now consider each of those squares or ice slabs a worth context. They are worth *everything* for one moment and *nothing* the next. To misunderstand their worth, by stopping, makes them worthless, even dangerous.

The ice slab, the friction handhold, and the squares on the checkerboard are momentary worth contexts—and cost has little direct relation. Many mountaineers would have paid fortunes for that one-beat friction handhold. Some people do spend fortunes on one short spin of the roulette wheel.

The Seasons of a Worth Context

As you well know, prices change constantly and not always upward. A ten-year-old car costs less than it did new. (A twenty-year-old car often costs *more. It has moved into a different worth context.)

What causes prices to change constantly is the growth or deterioration of a worth context. Toys that children crave are put on sale at 50 percent off the day after Christmas. Their worth contex* has peaked and fallen abruptly . . . A major client mentions that an employee you are about to fire was extremely helpful in their last project, so you reconsider the employee's worth context . . . The city council has decided to apply commercial zoning to some worthless land you sold . . . Your key supplier has a strike, and you turn to a second vendor that has had a "shaky history" . . . All these are changed worth contexts.

Even people have their seasons of worth. About fifty years in the work force, usually. Of that, the first ten years is energy without experience (largely wasted) and the last fifteen years is experience without energy (useful but lacking force). Ask anyone in personnel: ages thirty to fifty are when people's abilities are worth paying for. With better nutrition and exercise, experience without energy need not come so soon, but we've yet to find a way to give the young enough experience to use their energy wisely.

So what do you do with a worth context you know will change?

1. Forecast a Life Expectancy for that Worth Context.

Find its peak and downward slope, and plan to be in a different situation (or have a very good backup) when the worth context starts declining.

EXAMPLE: Job life spans . . . Most jobs have a period of learning and achieving, and many have some potential for growth. If you are hiring someone, you are wise to estimate how soon he or she will achieve proficiency, and how long he or she will stay productive before expecting growth, promotion, or another change. Many managers hire people who become proficient and productive only six months before their marketability has them looking elsewhere. Those managers should plan how to keep those employees or synchronize their hiring of new employees with the natural cycles through these jobs.

EXAMPLE: A piece of electronic test equipment may be the first of an evolving family of related products. You can predict that within six months there will be a better product for the same price, and the price of this one will go down. The worth context question is . . . What is it worth to you to use this equipment for the next six months? It may mean everything in a tightly competitive situation, where timing is the key. Six months may mean the difference between grabbing a worth context on the upswing and not grabbing it at all. Otherwise, you'd be smart to wait.

2. *Devote Extra Effort to Maximizing Productivity During a Worth Context.*

Certain profit centers in certain business have come to be known as "cash cows." In other words, if they are milked for all they're worth, they pay for explorations into other areas. Football, for instance, has long been a "cash cow" for some major colleges' athletic programs, which is why winning coaches and players are treated so well.

But "cash cows" are usually only a phase of a worth context, sometimes one which lasts only a short while.

EXAMPLE: When publishers create a new magazine, they expect it will take a couple of years to recoup their front end investment. Then the magazine becomes a "cash cow"—until new periodicals competing for the same readership and advertising are introduced. If the publisher is not aggressive in building circulation, increasing advertising, and maximizing profits during the "cash cow" period, substantial redesign and reinvestment will be called for when the worth context declines because of new competition.

To maximize the productivity of "cash cows," one has to:

-   –Accurately predict the cycle of the worth context.
-   –Have the capacity for milking the "cash cow" when its time has come. The most frustrating thing people in business encounter is not being able to borrow enough money to build up inventories for anticipated "cash cow" periods.

3. *Do Not Try to "Resurrect" a Worth Context When Its Season Is Declining . . .*

It is unlikely that any extra chrome or exciting ad copy will induce us into using hand-push lawnmowers again. Spending time and money trying to bring them back is a futile fight against a declining worth context. Their worth context could revive, however, with exorbitant gasoline prices and small lawns. *Then* someone with push mowers in stock could profit by a new worth context and its "cash cow" period (which will again decline with the advent of self-mowing grass).

Time as Context Versus Time as Cost

There is an important difference in common perceptions of time we should clarify here. Because we pay people by the hour, we have come to equate time with money. This practice, however, is only another version of piece work. The piece produced is an hour's work for, say, $10. Or a taxi meter running five minutes for $1. We do indeed "buy" pieces of time, but that is quite different from the time context we are speaking of here.

The *time context* is in effect our playing field. It has boundaries which are most often called "deadlines" but which we will call "futures," because they are worth contexts which extend from point to point in time. So when we speak of the *investment* of time, we are not speaking of the product for which we pay (an hour's work, five minutes waiting for a taxi) but of the apportionment of our clock to the various trade-offs we make.

It is true that we may pay to bring someone else into our time playing field (time context) to use it more efficiently, but to equate time solely with cost is to lose sight of the natural boundaries of a time context. Rockefeller with his millions could not alter the tides. And the ship sails at high tide, or it does not sail.

The Investment of Time

As a rule, time as a trade-off is more elastic than cost. Yet because of rhythms and cycles, we can often see the duration of any worth context—however spontaneous and short-lived—and work within it.

When we take clothes to the cleaners, we usually pay more for fast service than for service on the cleaners' regular schedule. We are then buying time, as the cliché goes. We are being allowed to use the clothing throughout more of their worth context by paying more money. But even if the fee were 5 cents, we wouldn't stand for six-month delivery. Perishable goods like food and film have a definite duration to their worth contexts, as do clothing and auto styles.

On the other hand, certain low-cost purchases, like land or hand-carved butter molds, will gain value if you can sit it out, giving them enough time to gain in value. We may die before hula hoops become collectors' items, but they *will* if we can only make enough room in the attic.

The latest lines of management thought on time management and long-range planning have coincided to allow businesses to choreograph both days and years in harmony with their own particular worlds. The reply to any failure not built into the plan as a contingency is that this was poor planning. So, consistent with its comprehensiveness, a plan should also build in failures, so that they too will be expected. Only failing to forecast failure is true failure.

To give both time management and long-range planning credit, they *do* allow us to examine future time trade-offs and perhaps avert poor ones. As you probably know, an early shipment can be nearly as bad as a late one because of high inventory costs.

As we've noted, there may be a *velocity* to events which increases at unplanned proportions. The upcoming competition which will doom your product may tell you that everything— quality and cost, and everything—should be sacrificed to selling that product in the shortest possible time.

The Analog of Futures

Beginning with *now* and ending with *forever,* we can envision an analog of times for forming worthy deadlines and making trade-offs.

Borrowing from computer science, when we use the word *analog* we imply a continuous measurement of a physical quantity. When weather forecasters say the temperature will go from 65° to 95° today, they are not saying it will go "zap" from 65° to 95°, but that it will gradually increase from 65° at the low end to 95° at the high end. Any thermometer is an analog device as is a car's speedometer or a slide rule.

Most light switches operate like the binary systems of digital computers. They turn "snap" on or off, not gradually. In the binary mode, you have 0 or 1, yes or no; the light is either all the way on or all the way off.

Happily, very few worth contexts act in a binary way. That is, rarely will something that was worth nothing suddenly become worth a fortune. Texas and Oklahoma dirt farmers might have had an inkling of changes to come when oil producers came around buying mineral rights. Changes in worth contexts often seem to occur on a binary scale because the increasing possibility of the change was ignored *until* it happened.

There are some of these, though, and when we hear about them, we sometimes feel the recipients of the windfall were less than deserving. Gold strikes in suburbs of Columbus, Ohio would be a "binary" change. We are sold insurance against negative binary changes such as fires, traffic accidents, and premature death. In fact, we couldn't buy very good insurance if its worth context were predictable. Try buying life insurance if you have a terminal illness . . .

Analog worth contexts are, on the other hand, the basis of our planning and scheming, and guide our actions in response to unknown future events. When we think of the "future" we are simultaneously thinking:

> Now, in a few minutes, tomorrow, next
> month, next year, two years from now,
> five years from now, the thirty-year mort-
> gage, the next century, and forever . . .

Each of us is a pioneer of time, and we are on the frontier of several "futures." Today is not only the first day of the rest of your life, but the first day of the rest of the week.

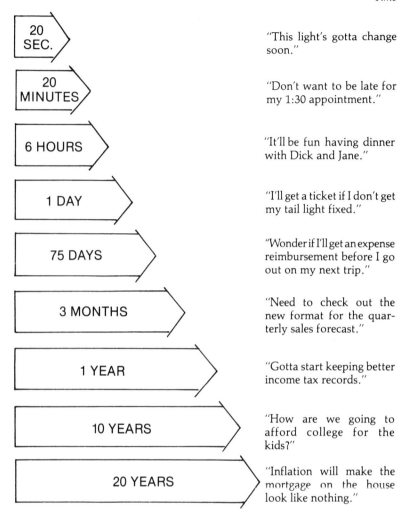

20 SEC.	"This light's gotta change soon."
20 MINUTES	"Don't want to be late for my 1:30 appointment."
6 HOURS	"It'll be fun having dinner with Dick and Jane."
1 DAY	"I'll get a ticket if I don't get my tail light fixed."
75 DAYS	"Wonder if I'll get an expense reimbursement before I go out on my next trip."
3 MONTHS	"Need to check out the new format for the quarterly sales forecast."
1 YEAR	"Gotta start keeping better income tax records."
10 YEARS	"How are we going to afford college for the kids?"
20 YEARS	"Inflation will make the mortgage on the house look like nothing."

Seeing time as an analog of futures means seeing that they are all happening at once. Some are just attached by a longer string, but all of them are pulling.

A good example for managers is developing people for greater responsibility. The short-term future may not seem to allow it. "Too much work. Can't let this person take on extra jobs or training right now." "Too much risk right now in giving this person more responsibility. Maybe later." But how long will businesses continue to trade off long-term development of people for short-term ends? Perhaps the answer is that there are few excuses for short-term failure and plenty to be found "out there" in the more distant future. Maybe when managers are held as accountable for long-term profits as they are for short-term results, they too can adjust their trade-offs. As it is, we rarely find managers who failed because they looked too far ahead.

But we do make some parallel trade-offs, *now* for an hour from now and *an hour from now* for tomorrow. "If I want to chat for twenty minutes I won't have the report done an hour from now (but maybe this chat I've been trying to have for weeks is a good time trade-off). I'll get the report in tomorrow morning before the ten o'clock meeting and do better next time. Of course, the matters in that report won't be on this week's agenda anyway, which means that decisions based on that report won't be made until next week."

But sometimes trading off a simple twenty-five minute future can be like needing the dish at the bottom of the stack. You want that specific one, but if you pull it out, down crashes the whole mess. It didn't *seem* to be that orderly a stack, but sure enough, take the dish you want now and the whole thing comes tumbling down. Sometimes in an organization, deadlines are like stacks of dishes. Mess up a crucial report and the five-year profit forecast (somewhere out on the other end) collapses.

What's needed is a runner's pace. A distance runner knows that he will have lots of energy at the start, but must hold back at first so that he hits the right check points at the right time to portion out valuable energy. Only by considering total time and pacing himself for the proper times between check points (not too fast, not too slow) can he hope to achieve a best overall time for his investment of energy. He is trading off a fast time in the first mile for a good time over ten miles. *Ten miles* is the worth context here, not one mile. That's management, envisioning the duration of the *total* worth context, having an exquisite sense of timing and momentum, and making trade-offs accordingly.

Twixtward Four

The three main concerns of the trader, then, are quality, cost, and time. The size of the angles in our simple triangle shows the relative importance of each factor balanced against the other two.

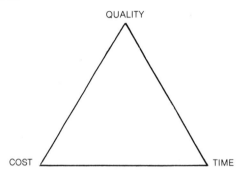

Before we move onto the trading ground, here's a capsule description of the tools we carry with us.

QUALITY

- Our perception of the difference between the actual and the ideal.
- Five levels—from *existence* to *validity* to *tolerance* to *fantasy bank* to *intuition*.
- Quality angle in trade-off triangle depicts variance from an ideal, so smaller angles represent higher quality.

COST

- A *balance point* between flows of worth.
- The *potential difference* between present and future.
- Either *protection* or *investment*.
- Creates and reflects a *worth context*.
- The larger the cost angle, the higher the cost.

TIME

- The *duration* of a worth context.
- Worth contexts have *seasons, rhythms.*
- *Momentum* matches velocity of actions to velocity of events.
- We are constantly placing worth contexts within an *analog of futures.*
- Larger time angles mean longer time or more time invested.

5

The Trading Ground

The sea-creatures that crawled onto land may have been the first life capable of a trade-off. In case no one's ever said it—thank you, creatures.

There are three kinds of people on the trading ground: those who know they are there, those who don't know, and those who have somehow forgotten. Those who have forgotten now take most of their trade-offs for granted, having settled on certain trade-off sets.

If we are in a position to make decisions about anything, then our constant habitat is the trading ground. We are always trading, and to do that well, it helps to know about all possible trade-off sets we can use.

Of course you've been to this trading ground before. We all have, all our lives. But just as every trip into new territory can benefit from a map, old territories become much more understandable with an overview of the terrain you've been seeing from ground level. Football coaches could not make good decisions without a spotter high in the press box, someone who has an overview of all positions. That's what we'll be attempting to do in this chapter—lift you away from the melee of your normal activity to see what the trading ground and its trade-off sets look like in the abstract. When you can see that, you should then be able to decide whether you want to change your trade-off sets and bargaining positions *and* recognize how to change them.

Here is a very simple example . . . drawn from the middle of the daily trading ground . . . a memo. *Should the memo be handwritten or typed?*

You have to decide between dashing it off in longhand or dictating and having it typed. You've probably been to the trading ground on this one a thousand times, but let's lift ourselves away and above it all for a second.

Option 1. A handwritten memo is low cost, low time, but low quality in appearance. We see this trade-off as:

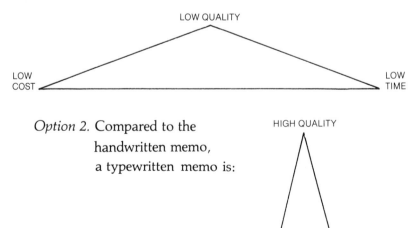

Option 2. Compared to the handwritten memo, a typewritten memo is:

You will of course decide this question in an instant, depending on the time you want to take and the impression you wish to make (and any governing protocol).

The point here is that all people are bartering with themselves *all* the time, trying to find an equilibrium in their trade-offs. All of us make our own individual trade-offs before we barter with someone else. Before we can look into the bargains we strike in accommodating other people's trade-offs, we must gain a much clearer and more distinct grasp of our own.

With most individuals, it's fairly easy to spot certain trade-off sets they prefer or tend to use as their *predecision-making postures.* Just as an individual develops an inclination toward certain trade-off sets, so do certain industries, professions, and other groups and enterprises. When you identify them, you can use and modify them and, if necessary, defend against these trade-offs when you really want something else.

Here are eight archetypal trade-off sets, presented in an order that may correspond to your sense of best and worst . . . or may not. Each is depicted by a triangle in which the size of the angles represents the importance of cost, quality, and time as desired outcomes of the trade-off. (The construction of the first trade-off set is as unusual as its occurrence in the real world!)

1. Low Cost—High Quality—Low Time

2. High Cost—High Quality—Low Time

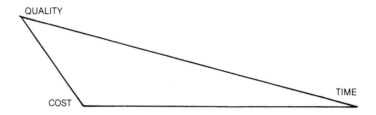

3. Low Cost—High Quality—High Time

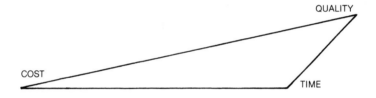

4. High Cost—High Quality—High Time

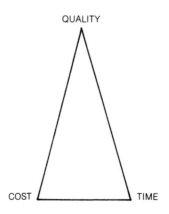

5. Low Cost—Low Quality—Low Time

6. High Cost—Low Quality—Low Time

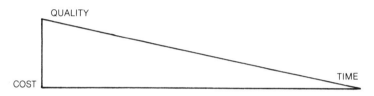

7. Low Cost—Low Quality—High Time

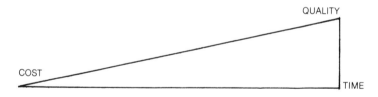

8. High Cost—Low Quality—High Time

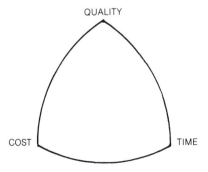

The Super Trade-Off Set

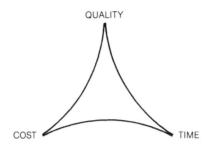

When we trade, we start by thinking of the best of all worlds, and we should start with nothing less. But balancing the highest quality against the lowest cost and time is rarely possible in the real world. Yearning for this ideal trade-off set drives people to pan for gold, court one-armed bandits in Reno, and pursue even wilder adventures . . . yet this ideal remains elusive.

Occasionally you will get:

A successful business someone wants to sell for $100 as a tax loss.

A coupon for two free meals at a restaurant you've always wanted to go to.

An oil driller who offers 50 percent of his earnings if he can drill on your worthless land.

Dream deals *do* occur, but they are certainly not usual events in our trade-offs.

No, the trading ground is a place where people come to exchange parts of this ideal for a part of reality. The trading ground need not be a place where dreams are shattered, but a place where distinct *actions* have this super trade-off set as a guiding principle.

The High Quality Trade-Offs

Human history is the history of a trading ground, where dreams (fortunately) give way to action. The diversity we see in human affairs results from *the way* that people—including ourselves—depart from the ideal of low cost, high quality, and low time. We will rank the other seven trade-off sets here on the assumption that most people (though perhaps not all) attempt to uphold quality by trading off for more cost, or more time, or both. So the most desirable trade-off sets would keep quality high, while making allowances on cost or time.

People upholding quality will trade off in one of these two ways:

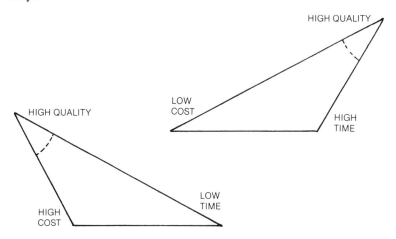

Suppose you are a shop supervisor dealing with a parts supplier. If you need a high quality part *quickly*, in order to meet production demands, you are probably willing to pay considerably more to get the quality you need today rather than waiting a week for the part to be ordered through normal factory channels.

Your trade-off set is:

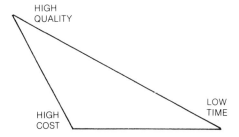

On the other hand, the special parts supplier has had this part on his shelf for six months, waiting for your need to arise. He, too, knew it was a high quality part when buying it wholesale, and he has waited a long time for you to walk in the door. His trade-off set?

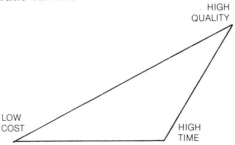

Much of the merchant's business sense involves perceiving quality *in the same way* his customer does, and trading off time until that right customer pays the price for the quality he wants now.

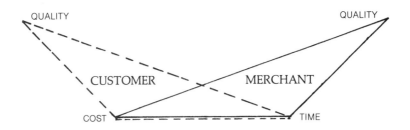

Either high time *or* high cost may be necessary to have quality. Sometimes *both* are necessary. That's when the cost trade-off set comes in.

A good example of this would be custom-designed office buildings. Designing a high quality building to your own specifications requires more time and money than building from standard plans and pre-fabricated parts.

For this high quality, which may provide prestige or serve a necessary business function, you will have to pay more and wait longer.

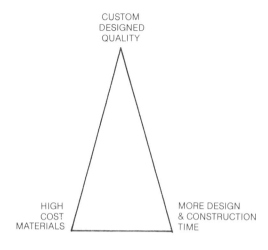

CUSTOM
DESIGNED
QUALITY

HIGH
COST
MATERIALS

MORE DESIGN
& CONSTRUCTION
TIME

There are four trade-off archetypes remaining, but first let's look at the three that revolve around quality. Here we hold our desired quality constant, while we trade off cost or time or both.

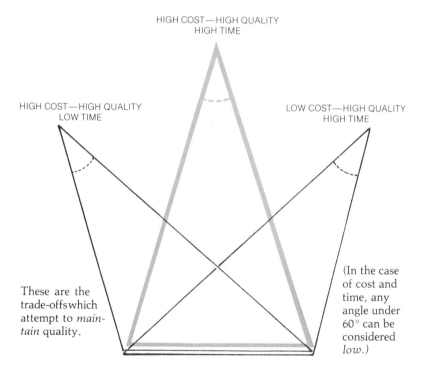

HIGH COST—HIGH QUALITY
HIGH TIME

HIGH COST—HIGH QUALITY
LOW TIME

LOW COST—HIGH QUALITY
HIGH TIME

These are the trade-offs which attempt to *maintain* quality.

(In the case of cost and time, any angle under 60° can be considered *low*.)

The Low Quality Trade-Offs

If you decide to sacrifice some quality, or don't consider it an issue, you still have some ways to do it that are preferable to others. One of the best would be:

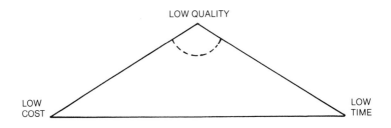

If you are forced to have low quality, why spend money or waste time getting it? On the other hand, if you only want to pay a little bit and need the thing in a hurry, can you reasonably insist on high quality? In any case, there will be times when low quality is inevitable, so your best trade-off is the one which minimizes cost and time. Same thing, when high quality just isn't important.

For instance, you may want to see a quickly typed draft of a letter so you can revise it. What you want is:

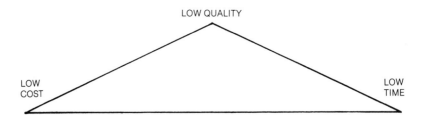

The best way to get the draft quickly and cheaply is to tell the typist it's just a "quick rough." Most typists will be able to go twice as fast if they can pay less attention to spacing and detailed correction of errors. If you do not say this, however, most typists will give you a quality job which takes longer. You'll get:

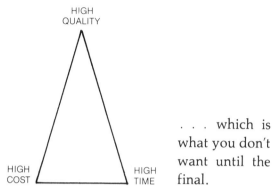

. . . which is what you don't want until the final.

You will find there are lots of occasions for less quality—many of them. So many that we have to choose the times we *do* hold quality constant in our trade-offs. One quality choice is medical care. People demand high quality medical care so regularly that it has become almost synonymous with high cost to the consumer. On the other hand, for our anniversary dinner we may select the best restaurant in town, but do quite well on peanuts and a soft drink for lunch.

The main reason we must *select* high quality "occasions" is that we cannot afford the cost or time it requires to have high quality all the time. Low quality goods and services are easy to accept when you demand immediate availability, of course. Fast food chains have catered to the low quality trade-off by offering their products at low cost and little waiting time. They are, above all, *available*.

In other cases we might not be so fortunate, and we'll get:

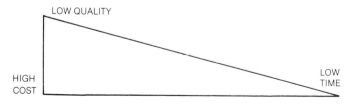

This is the operating premise for many small convenience stores. The quality of merchandise they stock is certainly not above average and their products cost 20–30 percent more . . . but they are quick. Lines are short and customers can have the one or two items they need in a few minutes and be back in their cars on the road.

Sometimes what you may be trying to achieve may be just so difficult that you put a lot of time in on it and it's still low quality.

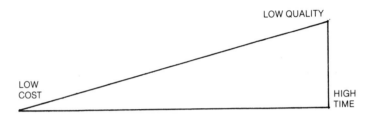

Or, more likely, you don't know how to make it any better.

EXAMPLE: Sometimes we try to get our cars running by replacing part after part, beating up our knuckles and bending our backs out of shape, and the damned things still don't run. (Which, if you'll recall, is only one quality point above their not existing at all. If your car still isn't running after you've changed every part in the engine, it is not what it purports to be.) How often do people who try to fix their own cars finally resort to:

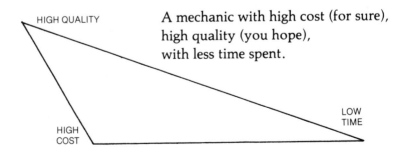

A mechanic with high cost (for sure), high quality (you hope), with less time spent.

The Big Loss

Carrying this last example to its awfulest conclusion, you come up with the "Big Loss" when either:

1. You spend a lot of time trying to do it yourself, ripping your knuckles off, before you take it to a high-priced mechanic who proceeds to do a lousy job.
2. You take it immediately to the high-priced mechanic who does a half-baked job and takes three weeks to boot.

Or worse, you finally get so fed up you junk the car and buy a brand-new lemon.

Any way you slice it, the "Big Loss" is a trade-off that looks like this:

You will, of course, avoid these situations on the trading ground as frequently as you aspire to the other extremity: low cost—high quality—and low time.

Trade-Off Preferences

Quality may not always be the most desirable choice. The way you order trade-off priorities depends greatly on your orientation, or that of your profession or company.

Obviously,

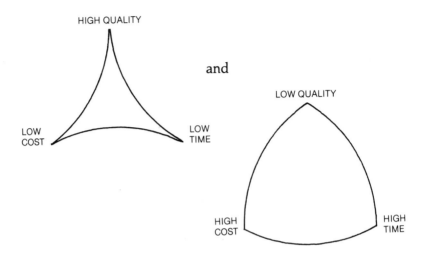

have got to be the highest and lowest priority trade-offs. In between, someone who faces constant deadlines (like on a
newspaper) might be inclined to trade off in this order.

Low Time—High Quality—Low Cost

Low Time—High Quality—High Cost

Low Time—Low Quality—Low Cost

Low Time—Low Quality—High Cost

Contrast how the preferences of someone who is extremely conscious of cost (a typical comptroller, for example) might go:

Low Cost—High Quality—Low Time

Low Cost—High Quality—High Time

Low Cost—Low Quality—Low Time

Low Cost—Low Quality—High Time

Shades of Grey

In our daily trading, of course, we do not just use the archetypal high–low sets of trade-offs. Between the two extremes (the highest highs and lowest lows), imagine the full array of trade-off triangles . . .

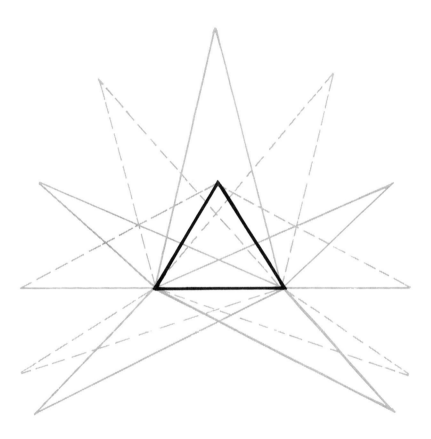

. . . representing infinitesimal variations in time, quality, or cost we strive for in our trade-offs. Dead center in that pattern is the average: medium cost—medium quality—medium time. So many of our compromises seem to strike for the medium, the trade-off that seems perfectly balanced.

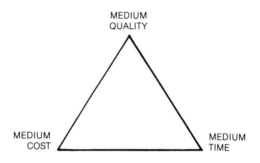

But when we start whittling, shaving, and bargaining, we find that we skew our trade-offs—be it ever so slightly—to favor cost or quality or time.

We know most compromises are either *just over* (more favorable than) or *just under* (less favorable than) an absolute average or "perfect medium." Smile as we may about "all parties being satisfied," we know someone usually walks out of that room a little more satisfied than someone else.

It's easy to see how we do this if we imagine our brains as a binary system of impulses. Each little switch is either on or off. Granted, when you have orchestrated 100 million possible combinations of "on" and "off," things may look a little grey. But down deep you win or lose. By degrees, granted, by infinitesimal degrees. But, finally, you win or lose. The light is on or off. You do not break even.

Managers are not much happier about breaking even than they are about ending up in the red. Overcoming inertia and doing *anything* to keep the universe spinning is enough to make us feel that we deserve to do better than break even. Equilibrium is the universe at rest, on quick freeze through eternity. And breaking even, for a manager, is losing quietly.

That is the "map" of the trading ground. It can be reduced to an intimate scale to fit your internal quandaries or your interpersonal trade-offs. It can also be enlarged to apply to divisions of a company competing for resources, to companies competing for markets, or even to diverse elements of society, such as government, church, and business, competing for attention. They are all on the trading ground, always.

For the moment, let's scale our thinking to you and the people around you, the traders you see daily on the trading ground.

Twixtward Five

Knowing the map of the trading ground means knowing the possible routes to achieving your best trades. Here is a new triangle to recap the possible extremes.

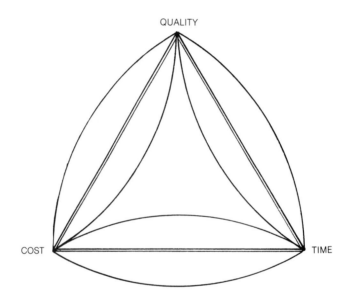

It displays all at once:
1. *The Best Possible* (low cost—high quality—low time) in the center,
2. *The Worst Possible* (high cost—low quality—high time) on the outside, and
3. *The Average* (medium cost—medium quality—medium time) between the two extremes.

Working from the average, we can see trade-off possibilities by modifying that average, *balanced* system.

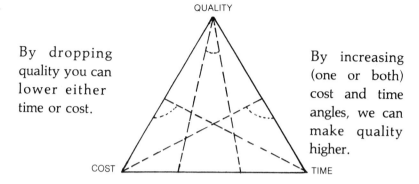

By dropping quality you can lower either time or cost.

By increasing (one or both) cost and time angles, we can make quality higher.

So the varieties of balance between factors "all of which are not attainable at the same time," become at once infinite and quite predictable. If one is to maintain quality, then cost or time get sacrificed. If one is in a hurry, quality may be shorted or cost may be high. And if one is cramped for pennies, quality or time will suffer.

How these balances affect people, organizations, and the cosmos is the theme of the rest of this book.

6

The Traders

The converse of Descartes' maxim is also true.

You have probably already formed a profile of yourself as a trader . . . . What do you usually trade for what?

Quality for time?

Time for money?

Money for quality?

And chances are you may begin to see some people around you for the kinds of traders *they* are.

   1. Does your boss not care very much about anything you do as long as you are at work on time?

2. Does the business manager sit on your reimbursement for a $500 sales trip because you are missing a $1.25 receipt for parking?

3. Does the advertising department add 25 percent to pad the budget for its campaigns because that's the only way they can be sure they'll get the quality they want?

You've been there . . . you can immediately begin to match people you know with these trade-off inclinations. But first . . . are you sure of your own?

Try this inventory. It won't be statistically valid nor will it fit your situation precisely. But it won't take long, and you may be able to see by the way you answer these questions, how your decisions can add up to a trade-off profile. The inventory is intended for you to examine things about yourself, but you could just as easily "take the test" for someone you know well.

TRADE-OFF INCLINATION INVENTORY

Directions: This short inventory is designed to let you form a view of your trade-off inclinations. For most people, trade-offs can change depending almost entirely on the unique circumstances surrounding them, or their influence on the decision to be made. This inventory asks that you avoid the natural "it depends" response by forcing you to pick one of three extreme trade-off positions in specific situations.

Check only one answer for each item. Remember this is an inventory, not a test. Precision in your answers and the profile they produce is not expected. Consider the simple situation posed in each item in isolation, then pick the one response most likely for you.

1. When you are dissatisfied with your job, what is the source of your dissatisfaction?

☐ lack of challenge   ☐ low salary   ☐ many extra or unproductive hours

2. You are asked to look into purchasing a new copying machine. What factor is most important to you?

☐ clarity of copies   ☐ cost per copy   ☐ speed of copy-
                                                         ing

3. You are product manager with a new product that has its best chance if it beats your competition to the market place, but then keeps a competitive edge with either higher quality or a lower price once you are both in. You can choose between two materials, a high quality X1 or a good quality X2. X1 costs more and takes longer to deliver. You can get X2 from two vendors: one who sells cheaply but delivers slowly and another who delivers quickly but charges more. Which would you pick first?

☐ X1   ☐ X2 with the   ☐ X2 with the
                               cheaper vendor   faster vendor

4. You must run 200 copies of a ten-page procedures manual for an important meeting next week. Would you . . .

☐ pay rush prices   ☐ have your   ☐ send the manual
for offset printing   secretary drop   to a quick-copy
and binding?   other work and   service?
                         make copies in-
                         house?

5. You must get agreement on a complex decision between four key people on a project by budgeting time next month. The peo-ple are located in New York, Los Angeles, Chicago, and Atlan-ta. Would you . . .

☐ fly them in for a   ☐ correspond by   ☐ have a telephone
one-day meeting?   mail?   conference call?

6. You have had several discussions with an employee about poor performance, which is reducing your operation's output, and you've even laid out specific expectations in writing. The employee still fails to perform even a small part of the job. Would you . . .

☐ spend as long as necessary getting him transferred to a job he can handle?

☐ fire him and hire an unskilled person to be trained?

☐ fire him and hire a skilled person who needs little training?

7. You are an aspiring product manager in a large, diverse organization and need a product to manage. Which of these products would you latch onto as providing the best use of your talents and the greatest opportunity for success?

☐ a high ticket, slow-developing prototype for competitive bid purposes

☐ a product foundering in high costs and low profits

☐ a product that taps a common technology that will soon be accessible to competitors

8. You must rent space for offices to augment those in your main plant. Would you pick . . .

☐ an attractive location ten minutes from the plant at $12 a square foot?

☐ an adequate location ten minutes from the plant at $7 a square foot?

☐ an adequate location five minutes from the plant at $13 a square foot?

9. You must buy equipment for an operation which will switch to newer equipment in six months. Would you . . .

☐ buy the finest equipment available?

☐ buy the least expensive equipment?

☐ buy the least expensive equipment with a ninety-day warranty if there are rapid service and replacement facilities nearby?

10. You are developing a training program. If effective, this program should result in less turnover and fewer grievances from employees. Would you . . .

☐ hire specialists to determine your company's specific problems, develop a custom design, and present the program?

☐ look for similar programs developed in the company in the past few years?

☐ buy the packaged program which seems closest to your needs and implement it immediately?

COLUMN Q

☐ (total number checked)

COLUMN C

☐ (total number checked)

COLUMN T

☐ (total number checked)

Scoring and Interpretation

After you answer all ten items, write the total number of checkmarks you placed in column Q, column C, and column T in the boxes provided at the bottom of the inventory.

If your score in column Q is seven or more, you are a chronic quality person. With four to six checks in the Q column, you will sacrifice a great deal for quality; and with zero to three, quality is often less important in your trade-offs than other factors.

If you marked seven or more in column C, you are probably courted by your banker but maybe not much loved by friends and employees. A low number (zero to three) in column C probably means you occasionally face budget problems.

A total of seven or more in column T suggests you have an acute awareness of wasted time. Zero to three, on the other hand, may mean you have trouble meeting deadlines.

If you like, you can make a pie chart to visually represent your trade-off inclinations. Make a circle and divide it into ten equal parts.

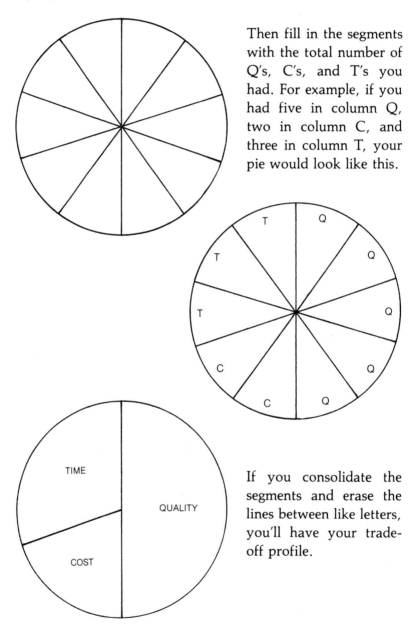

Then fill in the segments with the total number of Q's, C's, and T's you had. For example, if you had five in column Q, two in column C, and three in column T, your pie would look like this.

If you consolidate the segments and erase the lines between like letters, you'll have your trade-off profile.

This exercise can roughly identify and illustrate your basic trade-off orientation. The subtleties and nuances of specific circumstances cause you to alter your trade-offs every day, but this quick profile may help show where you (or some other people whose trade-offs you are trying to figure out) usually begin.

Now let's go on to flesh out the profiles for the three extreme trade-off inclinations. We'll talk about stereotypical individuals who seem to have *strong* inclinations toward one trade-off or another, though most of us have mixed concerns.

Notes on the Quality Person

A quality person will usually attempt to build quality into a product—even if no one notices—and to have quality things in his or her life.

The quality person sometimes is a nuisance to others when going way over budgets or blowing deadlines completely to "do the job right." On the other hand, this person can be *counted on* to do the job right if given the means and the time. Considering the few jobs that are done right these days, the quality person may be worth humoring.

Frequently, however, the pursuit of quality becomes a form of self-indulgence, a constant rationalization for having projects in late or for spending too much. The quality person's compromise in trading off bits and pieces of quality—in the interest of financial responsibility or professional punctuality—often comes very hard. Because high quality is held so dear in all of our "most desired" trade-offs, it falls even harder.

The good trader can offer the kind of quality that matches the situation. He can produce level A for $20,000, level B for $12,000, level C for $7,000, level D for $4,000, and level E for $1,000. And he says so to whoever is buying: boss, client, customer. The statement that all of such a range of products are first class is pure hooey. They are first class if the budget and timetable are first class.

In trade-offs affecting his quality of life, the quality person risks deep, long-term debt if he cannot determine just what *does* contribute to his quality of life and whether the same benefits can be derived at a B or C level of quality. Given identical incomes, one person may have a moderately priced home, children in private schools, and drive a used car, while another has an expensive home, a new car, and children in public schools.

"Wasted quality" is yet another pitfall the compulsive quality person faces . . . If everything in life must be high quality, it may lead not merely to high frustration if it cannot be achieved, but also to dulled appreciation when it can be. Quality overload may be comparable to too many rich foods in the diet. It is one thing to know what tastes good and another to be gluttonous.

Notes on the Cost Person

Foreigners often remark about how freely Americans discuss how much something costs, or how much money they made from a deal, or that someone has a six-figure income. To many foreigners this is impolite or, at best, a curious obsession of many Americans. What they don't understand is that our society suffers from a mania for keeping score. We count and rate and rank and figure practically anything.

Top tournament golfers
Stock performances
Best-selling books
Top-twenty records
Most goldfish swallowed in an hour
Winner of seven Oscars
Ten best-dressed women
Most headroom in a compact car
Lowest gas mileage
Highest energy efficiency ratings

We all keep score—on lots of things less silly than these—but the cost person is *obsessed* with scoring. Most of us have no trouble deciding we'll skip the side trip to Rhode Island when we're traveling from New York to Chicago, even if it is the only state we've never visited. Not the cost person . . . . Whether it's the number of grocery coupons clipped from newspapers, the number of states he's been in, or the appreciation in the market value of his house, the cost person is *always keeping score.*

Two unfortunate results that may come from being a cost person are:
1. He spends a lot of time *keeping score* or trying to score. The bargain hunter may be traveling hundreds of miles and spending countless hours, trying to score on $5 items.
2. He frequently loses all sense of quality—or even utility—as long as the price is right. His car may not run, but it was cheap. He may never need the stethoscope bought at a garage sale, but it was a steal. And he may confuse the end of a worth context (when costs decline) with a very good deal.

The quintessential cost person can, of course, be extremely valuable to a business, if what he produces is acceptable and takes a reasonable time. That same cost person can be counted on to support himself *and* a family, within the limits of his budget. His lights are on late as he balances his checkbooks, keeping track of these scores all the time.

Notes on the Time Person

The time person is extremely conscious of time contexts. To him, wasting time is a much greater failing than wasting money. Time is like land, "they just aren't making any more of it" as far as the time person is concerned. Some of this may reflect a fear that some worth context we don't know about could be slipping away, but the time person *feels* he will stand the best chance of grabbing all worth contexts if he does *everything* as soon as possible. In some circles, this time paranoia is called "the Jesus factor," which means you must always be a few minutes or days ahead of the time something is actually needed so you can be sure it's there and look like you-know-who.

It can be quite annoying to work with these chronic time people. For example, an important order must be delivered by March 15th, so the big boss says have it by March 12th, and your boss's boss says have it by March 10th, and so your boss says have it by March 8th. It's March 7th today, and you could easily have it without panic March 14th. But you *will* panic and you *will* have it by March 8th. That's the name of the game with time people.

Often we see employees playing a game called "high carding" to get these projects out "on time." One project that must be done immediately is from the division vice president. Then a different request comes from the president. This must also be done immediately. More immediately than anyone else's project. So the employee then has a high card to deal with the VP. When the chairman of the board comes in with an immediate task, the employee can "high card" the president. Usually, groups of employees carrying out the top executive's wish play the "high card" game. This is how priority ratings become deflated currency in many organizations: time people and their "Jesus factors" encourage "high carding" which, ironically, often results in delaying necessary tasks.

On the positive side, time people will get you to market before the market vanishes. They will get to work on time. And they will have reports on time. They really do live their trade-offs, and there are times when nothing—not high quality or low cost—is as important as being in the right place at the right time. The clock ticks on, and the worth context changes from red to black on the roulette table. If someone can tell us where to be with our chips when the wheel stops, cost will always be comparatively low—and quality, ours for the demanding.

Inclinations, Endeavors, and Circumstances

Although the variations in people, work, and objectives are infinite, it may be quite possible to extrapolate for yourself what these trade-off inclinations *might* indicate generally in terms of your compatibility with the type of work you do. Try this simple matrix of compatibilities of trade-off inclinations with types of work.

INCLINATION–ENDEAVOR COMPATIBILITY

	Industrial Functions	Retail Sales	Trades & Professions
Quality Inclination	Quality Control Product Design Advertising Merchandising Manufacturing Research & Development	Jewelry Furniture Clothing Automobiles	Architecture Medicine Law Communications Graphic Arts Writing/Publishing
Time Inclination	Marketing Public Relations Product Planning Shipping	Fast Foods Convenience Stores Fuel Supplies	News Media Transportation Construction
Cost Inclination	Personnel Purchasing Finance	Supermarkets Chain Stores	Accounting Banking Real Estate Investment Brokerage

Or perhaps it would be valuable to speculate on a typical question a person of each trade-off inclination might ask when confronted with a common situation at work.

INCLINATION–REACTION PROBABILITY

	Deadlines	Purchases	Procedural Change	Learning Situations
Quality Inclination	What doesn't have to be double-checked or tested?	Will it continue to hold up and serve us?	What are they compromising?	How will this help us do better work?
Time Inclination	How far ahead should the working deadline be to meet the real deadline?	What will we miss out on if it breaks down?	Will this take long to establish?	Will the time spent learning save time in the long run?
Cost Inclination	What is the penalty for missing this deadline?	Are there cost advantages to repurchasing?	Does this create or cut costs?	Does this apply directly to increasing capacity or demand?

These are, of course, only conjectural models, of limited accuracy and quite incomplete. But they may serve to help you develop more models in your own thinking.

Trade-Off Collision Courses

Differences in trade-off inclinations collide, not occasionally, but always. Even when you *can* analyze other people's actions in terms of their trade-offs, it may be hard to decide what to *do* with this knowledge of yourself and others. What two people hold in common usually presents the simplest resolution to trade-off collisions. In a way it's like playing "odd one out," but instead it's "odd trade-off out."

See if you can spot some typical trade-off conflicts you have had, or that you have seen between other people. The purpose of laying out these trade-off collision courses is to show some resolutions to what may otherwise be standoffs. Then we'll explore at least three "odd trade-off out" avenues which may provide a way out for the three major *conflicts:* cost versus time, time versus quality, and cost versus quality.

TRADE-OFF COLLISION COURSES

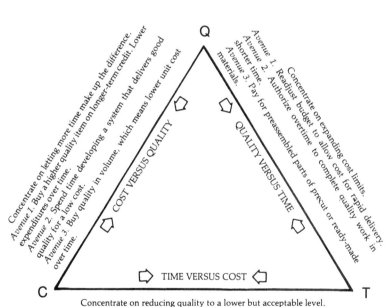

Concentrate on reducing quality to a lower but acceptable level.
Avenue 1. Use materials which work as well but don't look as good.
Avenue 2. Use methods which will narrow the scope of your service.
Avenue 3. Qualify "quality" claims with descriptions such as "basic," "functional," "useful," rather than "durable" or "beautiful."

Cost–Quality Collisions

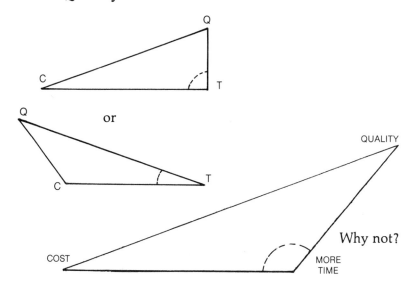

A cost–quality conflict can often be resolved by stretching cost over more time. For instance, car dealers and bankers came up with a clever way for new car buyers to afford more quality in a car than inflation seemed to allow. The solution? Longer-term credit. You pay less per month, but you pay *longer*. This solution can, of course, be applied to numerous business situations (e.g., longer-term rates on buildings and major equipment).

Another way that cost–quality conflicts (avenue 2) can be resolved is by taking time to develop a system that produces high quality at a low cost. Sometimes this involves delaying production schedules to achieve better product design. If time is not as important as cost or quality, time can be traded off.

A third way that cost–quality conflicts (avenue 3) can be resolved is by volume purchasing. If you can use the same item for years, then you can reduce the unit cost for the desired quality by purchasing a large quantity and receiving a volume discount. Your higher cost up front is then, in effect, a reduced cost over time.

*In exploring all of these avenues we are
talking about finding an immediate and acceptable trade-off for all parties, not about
a way to triumph with your own particular
trade-offs.*

Time–Cost Collisions

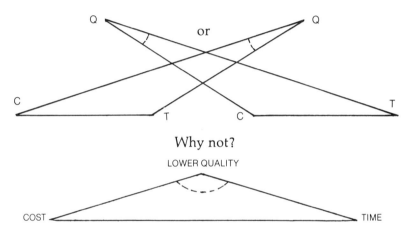

In time–cost conflicts we should concentrate on the question: "How much quality is necessary, anyway?" We can often
reduce some quality in our products or services in the interest of
lower time or costs and not sacrifice the basic *function* of the
product or service. For instance, a paperback book may have
the same quality of information as a hardback. But the cost of
manufacturing and the time needed are not nearly as high. So
one way of lowering quality within acceptable limits is to use
materials that function as well but don't look or feel as good,
reducing quality in appearance only.

In service industries you can reduce cost and time by
narrowing the scope of your service. Two ways come to mind.

1. Have the customer come to you. You save the time and
   cost of traveling to your client's work place. (Doctors
   rarely make house calls any more.)

2. Ask the customer to analyze the problem before you arrive. Much of a consultant's time and cost come from defining the real problem. (Problem identification questionnaires and trouble-shooting charts for car repair help narrow down causes before service begins.)

A third way of lessening cost–time conflicts by lessening quality is to lower the customer's expectations of quality. For example, you may call a product "basic," "functional," or "useful" rather than "durable" or "beautiful." You may call a service "diagnostic" rather than "complete." In either case, you intentionally lower the quality expectations of the customer. Then you lower your quality standards and presumably can reduce production time or cost or both. (Let's face it, if a customer only needs a small, push lawnmower to mow two square feet of grass, he may appreciate not having to buy an eight-horsepower riding mower with a chrome-plated engine.)

Quality–Time Collisions

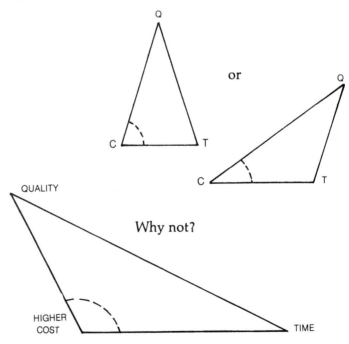

Concentrate on expanding cost limits for quality–time collisions. Money won't buy everything, although it may be legitimately used to reduce conflicts. If cost is not the major issue in a conflict, then proper *use* of a little more money can often resolve the issue. This is where you readjust the budget.

For instance, if a top-notch annual report must be finished by January 15th, it may be necessary to readjust the printing budget to allow two-day processing of color photographs taken at the last moment when a new product was released January 1st. Most things should be planned, but there are times when bona fide budget adjustments are called for.

For example, when a product is being rushed to market, paying overtime may be necessary to complete quality work within the time frame. A manufacturing supervisor may not enjoy deciding how many quality control inspectors to put back on the production line, a trade-off between time and quality. If she can pay overtime, she may be able to continue on schedule with the quality she wants.

A third way to resolve a quality–time conflict by concentrating on expanding cost limits is to use preassembled parts or preprocessed materials, and structure those into the cost of production. This is the basic "make or buy" decision for many managers.

Most computer firms and radio manufacturers, for example, don't *make* their own electronic components. They buy highly reliable ones from companies that mass produce transistors, diodes, and integrated circuits. Then the computer firms and radio companies simply use those components in a finished product, saving immense time to market while preserving high quality.

Those are just a few simple resolutions to one-on-one conflicts arising from trade-off situations. They *can* become more complex, but this chapter should encourage you to examine your own trade-off inclinations and to begin observing the inclinations of others.

There are also larger trade-off galaxies in which you may feel like a small trader indeed, subject to forces and changes that are unseen and that sometimes leave you . . . traded off.

Is being "traded off" just a matter of fate? Well, since these larger galaxies are also ruled by sets of trade-offs, we'd have to say "probably not." There are options for the galactic trader.

Twixtward Six

You are a trader among traders, and it is helpful to know if you are fundamentally cost-oriented, time-oriented, or quality-oriented. It is also helpful in your dealings to know the trade-off orientations of others.

There are three kinds of trade-off conflicts you may encounter: cost–quality conflicts, quality–time conflicts, and time–cost conflicts.

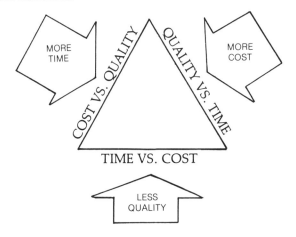

And, there are several solutions for these conflicts between well-meaning traders, in each case arising from the concept of "odd trade-off out." That is, given the trade-off *you* protect most, and the one the *other person* protects most, then your avenue out of the conflict is the *least* protected trade-off in your interaction. (Cost–quality traders should extend time. Quality–time traders should enlarge costs. Cost–time traders should lower quality.)

Before we consider more dizzying galaxies of human endeavor, please note that the individuals we have been discussing, the ones you deal with, may well be merely *representing* whatever their operation or profession usually trades off. Whether they (or you) are happy representing those operations or professions is a trade-off question of a very personal nature.

7

The Galactic Trader

How most of us make it through the saw-blades and steamrollers of life is statistically miraculous.

Even though you may be able to trade well in one-on-one situations, at several of life's junctures you may have wondered: "How did I get caught in these dead ends?" or "How did I get caught in the hot spots?" or "Why am I getting traded off here?"

The answer is simple. You are in a worth context yourself, and what you are selling has its seasons, too. In the last chapter, we discussed how you and someone else can resolve trade-off conflicts by an "odd one out" method. But, when trade-offs outside your sphere of influence are made, *you* may be the odd one out. So this chapter will be about:

Recognizing galaxies

Knowing where impact areas are

Your options as a galactic trader

Trade-Off Galaxies

As a child you may have thought of your address with not only your name, street, city, and state but with your country, continent, planet, solar system, galaxy, and universe. That address really shows that we are at the center of a set of spheres of increasing size. In a business situation, that "universe" (in which you are the shining sun) could look like this.

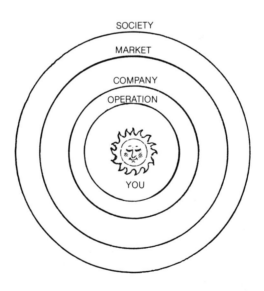

However, few of us can position ourselves well enough to have all spheres of influence so nicely concentric. We are fortunate, actually, to have as much alignment as this.

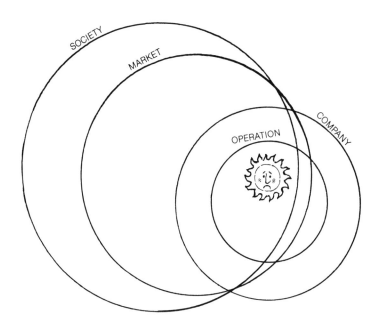

These circles illustrate the spheres of influence that affect you, and your position within them measurably affects what you can do and how effective you can be. The amount of overlap indicates how much of each sphere has influence on the other spheres. For instance, say the market for a new drug you invent fits with society's needs. Drug research is part of what your company does and part of what your operation does, and it is what you do entirely. You are in good alignment. Your worth context in relation to your universe is momentarily secure.

HOWEVER . . .

What if you don't discover a

competitive product?

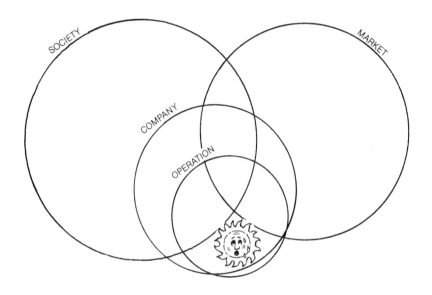

You are doing something *society* says is needed—drug research. Your *company* needs drug research. The *operation* needs a drug researcher. Yet you can't produce what the *market* requires. You have slipped out of a vital area, and your worth context is dimming rapidly. What can you do?

Or perhaps . . .

Your new drug satisfies market requirements, makes a profit, and your operation begins to mass produce it . . . but the Federal Drug Administration says it may be harmful in combination with certain foods—and holds your new drug for further study.

You are what your operation needs—a researcher; you do what your company needs—find new drugs. Your drug is competitive in the market place, but society says it may be unsafe. Your worth context is slipping.

In these two cases, your company or operation will probably not hold you totally responsible. Usually, reviews and "team" decisions protect you somewhat, and management then either changes the work you are doing or has you rework the product. Unfortunately, sometimes your whole operation slips out into the cold . . . while the project is suspended. That is why most operations have some "back burner" projects to move into in a situation like this.

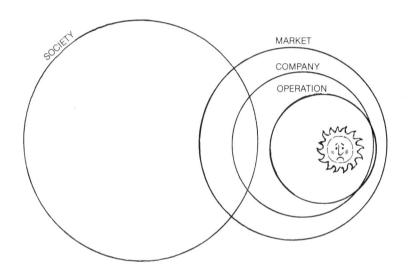

Business is not the only endeavor in which you are part of "society" or part of a "market." Anything you do has a worth context. In a government institution dedicated to eradicating a disease, for instance, you must look ahead. Once the disease is wiped out, you are not competitive in a market—there are no diseased people—and you do not serve a need of society.

Of course, the trade-off may be made *before* the disease is wiped out when, for example, a new administration decides the disease is well enough under control that your budget can be cut and the funds applied elsewhere. Not quite the same circles. You are still serving society, but your disease is of less concern to the market than a new, more exotic one.

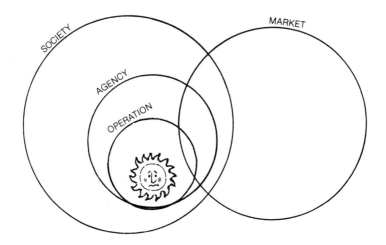

Even "fads" in government thinking can affect the worth context of your endeavor. If the popular issue this year is hydroelectric power, health programs may get traded off in the budget.

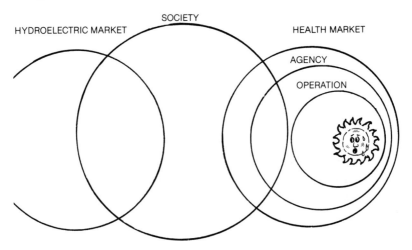

In this case, your whole operation may be traded off and you with it. You look for another job in an area that hasn't been traded off yet. But we often don't examine the probable life span of that new worth context and may be caught again. For this reason, it is good to monitor and forecast worth contexts closely from the beginning, since spheres of influence are always shifting.

The options that are open depend upon the season of the worth context you are in. If you are at its peak, you can use your present success to enter another worth context that is rising. If you feel the sun waning upon your efforts, you may be fortunate to find an operation (or company) at or near the peak of its worth context.

Worth Contexts and Your Personal Stock

You are, of course, concerned with trade-offs within your organization, at least to the degree they affect you. This is why we have been looking at various ways spheres of influence may shift and—without deliberate intent—lower the value of your stock, and perhaps even trade you off.

The galaxy which was at one time aligned like this,

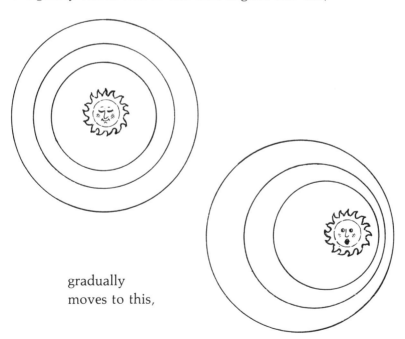

gradually
moves to this,

and then to
this,

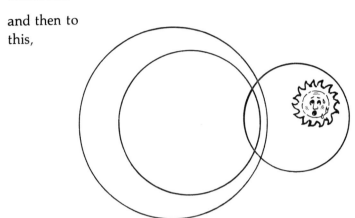

. . . finally placing you outside the worth context of larger
spheres. Then you can only hang on, as your operation makes
adjustments to move back into the market. If you do not
manage this realignment, the final alignment will look like this.
The galaxy moves on without you and leaves you aside.

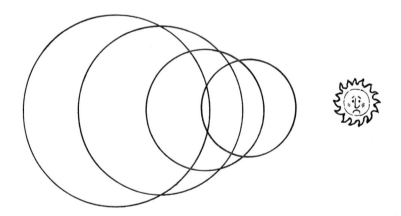

Your job survival depends on your perception of larger
trade-offs, those between society and the market, the market
and the company, and the company and your operation. For instance, can you foresee that the highly efficient operation you
are now running depends upon readily available energy that
doesn't increase in cost faster than inflation? By looking at the

larger trade-offs which are now being made—in federal regulations and consumer buying trends, for example—you may get an idea of the trade-offs you should start making, or realize that your present worth context may begin to decline.

Say your company division has been relying heavily on government contracts, with little emphasis on consumer market applications of the product you are making. Yet, by making slight cosmetic modifications, you might have a good consumer product. If Congress is considering a major budget cut in your general product area, that may be the first sign of withering contracts. And the person truly aware of worth contexts would be looking into how a consumer worth context might be served with the least changeover. The next sign may be trips to Washington by top executives in your division. They are obviously trying to hold onto a worth context that may be slipping. Here is what is happening:

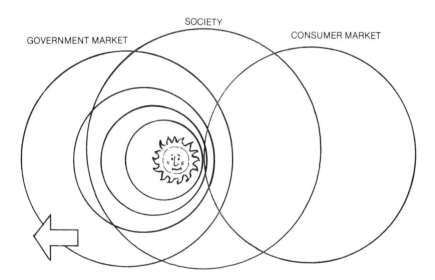

The government market may be slipping away, its worth context declining. But a consumer market may be waiting, its worth context rising. You may have to make a few minor trade-offs that help you step into that new consumer market. You may:

Trade off a little T.V. time to read more about new consumer trends.

Spend time at work preparing contingency plans for a move to the consumer market.

Calculate the costs of cosmetic changes that would help consumer marketability.

Decide what quality areas you could shave to accommodate the modifications.

List other areas that could change to your advantage (and disadvantage) when moving to the consumer market.

The person who is ready with answers to questions like these may be able to swing into the new worth context on the rise, changing direction with the spheres instead of being traded off.

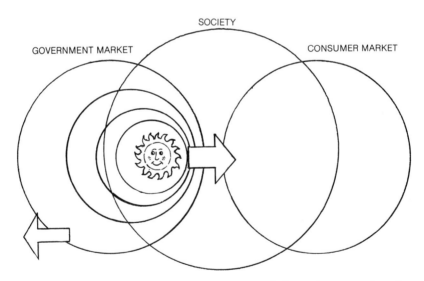

If you can observe the movements of the spheres and make trade-offs that *allow* a change in direction, your personal stock will climb. You will be in a growth position rather than in a declining worth context.

There is something else that strongly influences the value and growth of your personal stock, and that is the impact areas you choose to work in. These areas could be subcategories of the larger organizational trade-offs made as the spheres of influence change. But they definitely affect you, how you are treated, how you progress, and . . . how important you are. That, of course, is what governs all trade-offs, how important one element is in relation to others.

Impact Areas and Rankings

In many companies with highly sophisticated salary and administrative structures, a branch manager in sales not only has a job classification (sales manager) and a job grade (branch manager), but also an *impact ranking* which is usually kept secret from the individual and his or her peers.

This impact ranking has *nothing* to do with a person's capabilities or performance. It reflects, instead, how important his or her work is to the present aims of the organization. Therefore, an extremely capable manager doing superior work in a *low* impact area may not make as much money or have the job security of the barely capable manager doing a satisfactory job in a *high* impact area. This practice corresponds directly to the concept of a worth context: an impact ranking is a statement of present worth of an individual's contribution to the organization.

Sometimes companies will even formalize the impact ranking process so that every year top managers rate areas of activity as having A, B, C, D, E, or F impact on the concerns of the company that year. In these cases, the impact factor is figured in right along with performance and other factors in salary reviews and promotions. Because exact rankings are not usually disclosed below middle management, they are often the reason employees feel they are "going nowhere" but can't get any solid information on what to do about it.

Let's consider five important questions about impact area and rankings.

1. Why are impact rankings kept secret?
2. Do these impact rankings change?
3. Do all companies have impact rankings?
4. How can you predict and shift to new impact areas?
5. Do you want to move into a high impact area?

Why Are Specific Impact Areas and Rankings Kept Secret?

Assuming there *are* specific rankings (many companies are governed by managerial whim), these are seldom made clear to employees because they drastically affect pay. Announcing impact areas could mean a heated race to get into a high-ranking one, or a great deal of haggling (including court cases) over whether that area really deserves a C, D, or E ranking. In the best circumstances, full disclosure would be seen as rating people's worth to a company, which could cause lower motivation and greater turnover in low-ranked impact areas even though these areas may still produce a solid profit or contribute in other ways to a company's well-being.

Do Impact Rankings Change?

Yes. Frequently. And usually their change is somewhat predictable. Impact areas that could be known in advance evolve from research and development and fill a consistent and lasting need in the company, market, and society. For example, solar energy product development is a fairly predictable high-impact area. On the other hand, if 99 percent of the toothpastes on the market are found to cause cancer, and your small, unimportant operation in a company that produces toiletries is making a cancer-free toothpaste, your impact ranking could be raised immediately. That worth context will last until there are other safe toothpastes again, and may last a good while longer, if you've used the image to establish a niche in the market.

On an A–F scale of impact ranking, the C level probably has the most predictable growth potential. It will predictably move to a B ranking and perhaps A. On the other hand, an impact ranking of D, E, or F usually designates an area which will be phased out unless—as in the case of cancer-free toothpaste—the unpredictable occurs.

Do All Companies Have These Impact Rankings?

You'd better believe it. Although most companies do not have formal A–F impact rankings in their pay structure, all companies do have identifiable impact areas. In fact, it is difficult to imagine a human endeavor which does *not* do impact ranking. Whether or not this ranking is explicitly stated, *every* manager of *any* group at one time or another, in one way or another, asks: "If there were a fire, and I could save myself and one other to continue this work, who would it be?" The next question is "Who would the second be?" and so forth. That is impact ranking, and it happens whether finance committees are reviewing new capital expenditures or managers of a unit with declining sales are deciding who to lay off. Impact rankings may seem cruel, but every organization finds them necessary and inevitable.

How Can You Predict and Shift to New Impact Areas?

By watching trade-off galaxies and aligning yourself with upcoming impact areas. There are stockholders' reports, growth of market share reports, all sorts of indicators available to anyone. With them you can take a proactive stance and recognize far ahead of time your impact area's life span.

Just as surely as you *realize* a brick is falling and take *action* to move out of the way, you also realize something is happening to society, the market, the company, or your operation. *Not taking action*, once you realize the larger trade-off which is being made, is one of your choices. Our not being aware of all our choices, however, is why we occasionally feel we have been "traded off," rather than having had something to say in the matter. One of the first choices was to watch larger trade-offs being made and to gather enough information to choose an action. Sometimes the person who learns Spanish when she sees a government trade agreement signed with seven Latin American nations has taken early action to improve her choices later. Knowing Spanish, she would then not have to trade off time and cost to learn it when the opportunity for branch management in Colombia arises.

The alternative to being actively aware of new impact areas in your organization is to judge your impact ranking by the "position of the sun." Common sense will tell any trader the position of the sun. Do you feel warm, secure, needed, sought out, listened to? You know when the sun is warm upon your back and when you need a jacket. Most of us can tell when we are being traded off. We just hope we can be comfortable a little longer. Then we get traded off for certain.

Many companies *want* people who try to determine impact areas and move into them. This management philosophy, sometimes known as "up or out," asks for the drive and initiative with which a person finds and edges into an impact area. Usually this also is the best indicator of who will produce well in the impact area where it counts most. Conversely, the best natural selection of the business world comes in trading off the ones who *should* be traded off. As the theory goes, a company becomes less competitive and may itself be traded off in the market if it does not make effective trade-offs with employees. That is most often done by impact rankings.

Do You Want to Move into a High Impact Area?

A good question, because there are advantages and disadvantages. An advantage is the warmth of the sun—all the resources you need and everyone noticing your performance. It is the high road to promotion, fame, and fortune. It is the place where bright ideas germinate and exciting decisions are made.

A disadvantage is that any poor performance is also noticed. For that reason, you may work harder and under more stress in a high impact area. As surely as you develop your operation to run smoothly forever, its impact ranking will decline.

Many people prefer to be on the periphery. Many people in C impact areas, such as staff jobs or support functions, can continue securely and happily for an occupational lifetime. But they will never be "B's." As generations of sales managers, coaches, and generals have said: "No guts, no glory." So being or not being in an impact area is a choice you must make, and other trade-offs fall into place with that initial choice. However, there are options available *within* that critical choice.

Options of the Galactic Trader

When we look out at the night sky from our dark trading ground, it seems as though distant galaxies are cold and unapproachable. As the ancients knew, those large systems directly influence us. And we travel within those galaxies throughout our working lives, so we should keep track of our options.

Maneuvering into Favorable Circumstances to Achieve

Most successful people will tell you that the most difficult part of their achievement was getting into the right position to *begin* achieving, into the galaxy and impact area which offered a rising worth context that needed their abilities. Finding this "right" worth context is difficult enough for most, although moving into it seems quite natural: only those who have the ability to succeed within that position bother trying. The odds for success once a person has maneuvered into the position are then extremely high (which is as it should be).

If you are certain your abilities tend toward a certain kind of work, you have two main options:

> Improving yourself outside the worth context, then moving into it.

OR

> Concentrating your efforts on getting into an impact area, then "hanging on" while you learn.

In taking the first option, you might study on your own, take courses, or gain experience in that area on or off your job. There is one problem with building up "background" knowledge and skill, however. Most "authorities" will not admit you are ever *quite* ready enough through education or related experience on the side. Unfortunately, the only real way to be qualified for a task is to be doing it. We have all known potentially brilliant writers, dancers, even managers, who thought they would first get "a little more education" and haven't really launched their careers.

The second option may take a lot of sheer gall. With it you edge—unqualified—into an impact area. But in the long run this may be the best way. Few people can ever be considered "qualified" for a position they move into. If they are, we might easily wonder if they hope to rest comfortably on their laurels. The best achievers are usually "semiqualified" people with initiative, who learn the task but also *shape* the task as they go. Thus qualification for any position might be considered half background and half creativity.

Most people don't know this. Most people think you become "qualified" by education and experience and are placed (from on high) into your proper niche. For those who know that most "qualification" takes place on the job and forms around what you achieve in that job, the world's opportunities lie wide open.

After all, who "qualified" the Wright brothers to fly?

Selecting an Achievement Style

For purposes of impact ranking, most people can be classified either as *managers* or *individual contributors.* A company lawyer may be an individual contributor having the same salary and influence as a manufacturing manager who is responsible for the work of a thousand employees.

One key decision in selecting an "achievement style" is whether to take the manager or individual contributor route. Quite often an outstanding individual contributor is asked to manage other individual contributors. Many professionals who have done well in the individual contributor role find they do not like management and go back to being individual contributors as soon as possible. One flaw in traditional corporate thinking is that managerial success is the only true success. That may not be true any longer, even in monetary terms. In many companies, individual contributors are given high status and pay for their ability to provide creative thinking and crucial direction to management.

Another choice in "achievement style" concerns working relationships. Even if you are dead right, you can railroad measures through (and be either a hero or a goat) or you can *spread* the credit and the blame. This is never an easy decision. Often a project takes longer if you try to get solid group support, much less unanimous agreement. On the other hand, if you do it all on your own initiative, the style you use in getting things done can affect the continued impact you may wish to have. Real producers continually weigh time against the quality of product or process resulting from unanimous support.

Deciding When You Have "Enough"

A pleasure of modest success is deciding when one has "enough"—responsibility, power, wealth, achievement, and so on. If most of us didn't reach some decision about this, and use our perception of "enough" to guide us and anchor our futures, people might be fighting more wars than they already do.

It is not difficult to imagine a society even more aggressive than our own, in which people constantly collide and claw out every morsel of achievement however that achievement is defined. Yet the option for each of us in life planning, or at any plateau of achievement, is to say, "Enough. I am satisfied. I am happy. I am complete. I am no longer in process."

When a person says "enough," he or she begins to seek more balance in trade-offs. This is a characteristic we see within operations, companies, markets, societies, and in whole cultures. The main alternatives are:

> Saying "enough" before our larger galaxies—operation, company—say "enough."

Contenting ourselves to be aggressive and productive within a galaxy which has itself said "enough."

Most desirable—finding a galaxy where the idea of "enough" is in harmony with the movement of your spheres. Add that to the definition of heaven.

Individual trading is a continuous process, whether with others or while being galactic traders, discovering and rediscovering our directions through the vast galaxies which shift constantly and urge us to reexamine our own trade-offs. When we do, we may find that certain trade-off sets we use are traps, while others can furnish opportunities.

Twixtward Seven

We are part of awe-inspiring galaxies, and yet we can feel marginal to them, watching the way they can sway our lives. Galaxies of human endeavor overlap and are part of larger galaxies, and within those systems of eternal flux, you are a lone galactic trader.

Ideally, you are in perfect phase . . . BUT

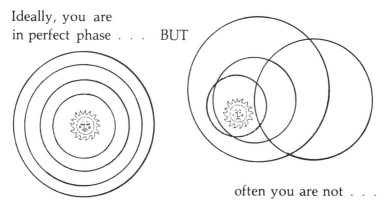

often you are not . . .

You trade and avoid being traded off by watching the movement of the galaxies around you. Being in good stead with these galaxies is not only a requirement for achievement, it is necessary for survival.

But once you are cagey enough to survive, your next concern will usually be finding the best position from which to enjoy that survival. You may desire to position yourself in a high impact area crucial to the direction your organization is taking, or you may be more comfortable on the periphery, where the pressures are not so intense.

Further options you have as a galactic trader include maneuvering to a position where you feel qualified, selecting your achievement style, and deciding when you have achieved "enough."

But we can also operate more effectively if we see where the trade-off traps lie and know how to avoid them or how to climb out of them far enough to view the horizons of opportunities.

8

Trade-Off Traps

---

*The fox who caught his tail in a trap
assured everyone he was in ecstasy.*

—*An Aesop paraphrase*

Inflation is one obvious example (though not the only one) why we should *suspect* many comfortable trade-offs of being traps. When we consider losses from savings accounts (or the savings possible by borrowing money today against tomorrow's inflation), it suggests that any security we have probably comes from our ability to recognize future worth contexts and to change our trade-off patterns in view of these contexts.

Starting on a path to success by making the trade-offs we feel comfortable with can help us avoid serious losses. Attempting the more difficult route of changing some of our trade-offs will surely help prevent us from falling into trade-off traps—those trade-offs we usually consider "fixed." Ridding ourselves of fixed trade-offs may mean more than gaining a more open view. It may offer opportunities we had not seen before.

The golfer whose ball lands in a sand trap does not revel in how close his shot came to the hole, since he must get out of that trap to reach the green. But the difference between a duffer and a pro is the pro's ability to "explode" out of a sand trap in a way that causes the ball to land not only on the green, but near the hole. The *only* way a trapped golfer can achieve this feat is to consider the escape from the trap as an *opportunity*. If he thinks in two stages, (1) getting out of the trap, then (2) putting from *wherever* he lands, he may find himself in a trap on the other side.

The first step toward trade-off opportunities, then, leads directly from trade-off traps. Trade-off traps are trade-offs we perceive as fixed but that really aren't. These fall into a few broad categories:

> *Structures*—rules, policies, practices, traditions which you did not devise and to which you never fully agreed.

> *Commitments*—agreements you have entered into with others, or your obligation to a series of trade-offs.

> *Habits*—personal time trade-offs which avoid excessive preoccupation with trade-offs.

> *Conventional Wisdom*—the attitudes and beliefs of others, which taint our very perception of the world.

Structures

Structures are often more flexible than other traps, because you may find that you can stretch or "interpret" their meaning to your situation and make them into opportunities.

The "most fixed" structures are physical structures. If you are not limber and athletic, making the next Olympic team might not be the right cause for trading off money (your job) for training time, because your quality as an athlete cannot be substantially improved no matter what you trade off. There are so few physical barriers now compared to the number we considered fixed in the early 1900's. Our country's limited possession of gold is no barrier to the amount of currency in circulation, and distance is less of a time barrier. So even these most fixed structures, physical ones, can and do change.

Rules are structures that some people have agreed to, but probably not you. Breaking or stretching rules is our way of modifying them so that we *can* agree to them. We may agree that having a federal income tax is a good idea, while scouting for every loophole—taxing the system in our own way.

Most rules are capable of being modified. There may be a law against driving on the shoulder of the road. But in a traffic jam many people keep moving, at least to exit ramps, by driving on the shoulder. They amend the law to say " . . . except in cases when the flow of traffic in the usual lane is stopped for over ten minutes." They may even make extensions of those amendments like " . . . at speeds of no more than fifteen miles per hour." The amendment and extension observe the *intent* of the original law, made to keep people from whizzing along dangerous shoulders. If people driving in heavy traffic did not bend the law, they could be late for work and have to decide between leaving early or living closer to work. By modifying the rule they avoid such a trade-off trap.

The same may be true in a company which practices zero-base budgeting. Theoretically, by company rules, any excess budgeted funds at the end of a fiscal year are turned back to general funds. Look at it from the manager's view (if you haven't had occasion to). With excess funds at the end of the year and a project to finish a month later, the manager can buy supplies and services now that can be applied to completion of the project. If the zero-base rule were followed strictly, the trade-off would have to be:

"Pay whatever is necessary to finish by July 1."

(And there is always a good chance of receiving no funding at all after July 1.) By *interpreting* the rule, the manager is actually completing the project in his or her charge, and doing so without increasing cost.

Policies are rules that are acknowledged as flexible. Salespeople can grant certain discounts for volume or timely ordering, and if the rule were too fixed, the competition would be in a better position to grab some of their business. So, based on experience, the company sets a "range" of price discounts depending on circumstances. The policy then allows salespeople to discount prices, say, from 2 percent to 5 percent at their discretion. Since policies are designed to allow interpretation, they are thereby open to further interpretation. If a sales representative lands a nation-wide Sears account, the sales manager would probably *expect* her to reinterpret the range, offering Sears up to a 10 percent discount for the volume that account would offer.

When structures seem to hold out only fixed trade-offs, they act as traps. But they need *not* trap you if you can conform to the intent of the structure while stretching it to allow the trade-off patterns you need.

Structures are most often modified because of an opportunity. We usually stretch rules and reinterpret policies because an opportunity looms on the horizon.

Commitments

Commitments are trade-offs to which you have actively agreed, either by *contract* or by *implied understanding*. "I'll have this to you by 4:30 P.M. Friday" is a *contractual* commitment. If you work for a company where work begins at 8:30 A.M., accepting a job there *implies* your commitment to be in around that time every day, or that your few exceptions will be justified.

These trade-off traps are often harder to break out of than any others, because you have a stake in your commitments, and they create a fabric of trust between you and your world. Occasionally, you will have to allow insufficient time on a project you wanted to do—even if its quality suffers—because you are committed to giving a report on the previous project at 2:00 P.M. next Friday. Or you pass up a chance for a better-paying job in another city because your kids are in school and you're enrolled in an MBA night program. Whether a commitment began through contract or implied understanding, it may be considered *inertia* as long as it remains unexamined. Many businesses count on inertia, along with reasonable job satisfaction and other factors, to keep employees who might otherwise leave for more pay.

But maybe the school is awful and the kids hate it, and you could find a better MBA program in the new city anyway. Don't always assume commitments to be stone solid or even to *be* commitments. Especially when they alter your potential trade-offs so drastically. The first thing to do is to check whether the trap you are in is:

Really a commitment or just inertia.

Really a better set of trade-offs than you might experience elsewhere.

Inertia can be overcome and commitments can be renegotiated. If you are in a commitment trap, examine the *strength* of the commitment and renegotiate it with the other people involved. Sometimes you may make a quick call the day before and say, "Remember we said 4:30 P.M. Tuesday for that material? Think you could give me until noon Wednesday, or is someone waiting for it Tuesday?" Occasionally, just stretching a deadline on a commitment will give you the ability, say, to fill a small order in a hurry for a potentially big customer.

Commitment traps can also result from a *series* of linking trade-offs between you and others. Usually that means you see your fixed trade-offs to be a function of:

> *What has happened previously*—because one trade-off set inclined toward one trade-off earlier, another trade-off set must now make up for that.

> *What is happening in parallel*—such as two or more operations trying to reach the same point at the same time or trying to *avoid* reaching the same point at the same time.

> *What you desire to be a future trade-off position*—trading off one element now so you can opt for it later.

Let's take a closer look at these traps.

Effect of Previous Trade-Offs

If a valuable employee has resigned who was worth much more than what she cost because of her experience, you may be in that position because you chose not to pay more and not to train a replacement. So now, it may take

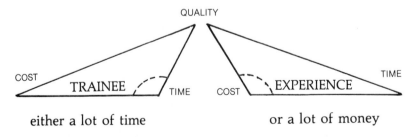

either a lot of time   or a lot of money

to come up with as productive an employee again. Because you committed yourself in one way earlier, you seem forced to be committed to another trade-off now.

When we avoid a trade-off at one point, we may have to come back later to rectify it with a different kind of trade-off than we might have liked.

Effect of Parallel Trade-Offs

When two operations are attempting to reach a point at the same time or (in the case of airplanes landing) are trying to avoid being in the same place at the same time, trade-offs may have to be taken in parallel.

For example, if two plants of the same company producing the same product at the same quality make different trade-offs, one for lower cost and one for lower time, then

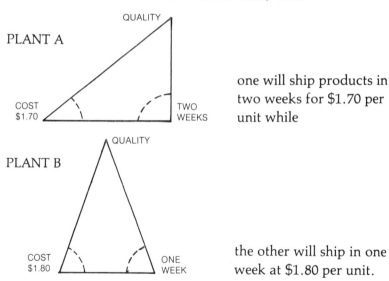

one will ship products in two weeks for $1.70 per unit while

the other will ship in one week at $1.80 per unit.

In this case, buyers may question this disparity between two plants of the same manufacturer. The two plant managers may be asked by the sales department to get their act together . . . to make their trade-offs match. Then, they would be trapped by a commitment to work in parallel, though this wasn't in their plans.

Effect of Future Desires

For the good pool player, scoring one shot isn't enough. You need to continue scoring on subsequent shots, and so must be as concerned with where the ball lies for the next shot as you are with scoring now.

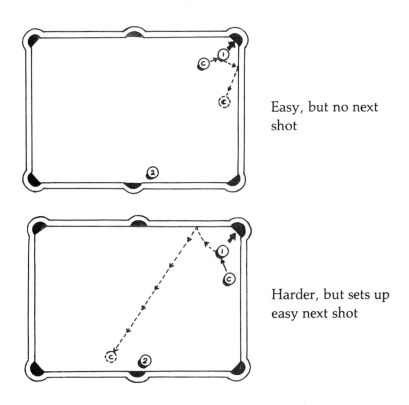

Easy, but no next shot

Harder, but sets up easy next shot

In the same way, our future desires affect the trade-offs we make now. For example, some companies will invest a certain amount of profits in long-range planning even if they need to expand now to produce enough for present markets. They know that if they do not have new products and markets at the end of current worth contexts (they all end), then they could be in as bad a shape then as they are in good shape now. Long-range planning is their way of putting the right English on the ball so they can run the table.

All these situations—past, parallel, and future—form sticky commitments that are difficult to break without violating trust or operating poorly. In some cases, the commitments must simply run their course, and you will try not to get in that position again. At other times, you may have to strive to *abandon* commitments before they totally detract from trade-off opportunities. In any event, a few unwanted but locked-in commitments should make traders wise to making commitments which severely hamper their ability to rethink and change their existing trade-offs.

The effects of previous trade-offs, parallel trade-offs, and future desires may commit you to a given trade-off now. You are well on your way to blasting out of the trap when you can project your future trade-off positions from the trade-off you are making now.

Commitments are reevaluated or changed either because of an opportunity that exists or to *allow* opportunities that might not have existed.

Habits

Habits form our line of defense against the toil of examining the trade-offs for each miniscule event in our lives.

Once we are in the habit of buying one morning newspaper, we don't have to decide between papers or whether the cost and time heighten our quality of life by providing us information. If we dutifully reconsidered our route home, preference for coffee with or without cream, use of paper clips or staples, or a thousand other little habits, we would be enslaved by trade-offs.

When Big Brother said, "Freedom is slavery," in the novel *1984*, George Orwell was not just toying with us. The compulsion to make a considered choice in every small matter is indeed a kind of slavery or, at least, an indulgence.

Nobody does this, of course. But we all have habits that do deserve examination in light of the trade-offs we are making: holding your all-staff meeting religiously on Mondays at 2:00 (whether you need it or not, no matter what else is happening) or writing letters versus using the telephone. The habit of having long, unorganized discussions at weekly meetings can, if curtailed, provide opportunity for detailed problem solving (or for a shorter meeting). But the trade-off can't be made if the habit continues.

Here's a good exercise. Each month, identify and evaluate the trade-offs you are making in maintaining a given habit—or do this whenever a circumstance arises that makes you go to some trouble to maintain a habit. Remember habits are for your benefit, to free you from having to make constant, inconsequential trade-offs. If they don't free your mind, or if they take too much time or cost to maintain, reexamine the trade-offs.

Habits tend to inhibit the search for better opportunities, and, in some cases, freeing oneself from a habit is necessary for a trade-off opportunity.

Conventional Wisdom

Perhaps the most pervasive and possibly the most inhibiting trade-off trap is the belief that the majority must be right, and that the more overwhelming that majority is, the more correct it must be. We allow conventional wisdom to fix our trade-offs so often that simply seeing it for what it is (which we hope you'll be able to do hereafter) may open vast landscapes of virgin possibilities.

Sometimes conventional wisdom is mistaken for "common sense," but that's not what it is. *Common sense* is native good judgement, such as, "I'm not going to jump out of that airplane and go hurtling through the air from 30,000 feet. Common sense tells me *no*."

Conventional wisdom, on the other hand, is simply conformity in thought. Here are some examples of past conventional wisdom.

"Social security will always work well, with the large number of young people contributing a little to support the few old folks left after retirement."
(This seemed plausible from what we knew of history . . . But now, with more old folks and fewer young folks?)

"A woman's place is in the home."
(There was a time when this served society. Now . . . all bets are off.)

"Invest in blue chip stocks, and you'll always be ahead of inflation."
(We didn't hear this much after 1974.)

"In a thousand years we won't have enough to feed the U.S. population."

(This last bit of conventional wisdom dates from just a few years ago. It is still held by some who don't know that birth rates are stabilizing and numerous food sources have been discovered. In the case of social security, society's conventional wisdom resulted in a series of linking trade-offs from which the system can now barely extricate itself before it goes bankrupt.)

It is worth the time to consider how conventional wisdom urges us into trade-offs that may really be disadvantageous. Look at those examples of past conventional wisdom and think about how *you* would have seen the trade-offs during those times. Fixed? If so, you are probably still bound by one conventional wisdom or another. Let's consider a few pieces of conventional wisdom in vogue right now, to see how we view them as fixed for trade-off purposes, and how they might be wrong.

"Employees work better if their problems are listened to and understood by their manager."

Or this one:

"Detailed long-range planning is necessary for the success of any business."

Or this one:

"It's better to buy a new car than to pay less for a used one and inherit someone else's problems."

TIP 1. Beware of Conventional Wisdom!

By the time two billion people think it's right, it has probably become wrong.

Let's take an unconventional view of this current conventional wisdom.

1. "Employees work better if their problems are listened to and understood by their manager."

What if this is wrong? What if this encourages people's natural inclination to revel in the attention of their supervisors and to bring supervisors more problems (even if they have to create them) rather than showing more *successful results?* This is not begging a question. If we accept this conventional wisdom as "fixed," we may be rewarding nonproductivity. If it is wrong, our trade-offs of high cost and time involved in this "fixed" precept of human relations (everyone's problems must be solved) may be high cost and high time for a low quality job. It's about time we consider an unconventional view here.

2. "Detailed long-range planning is necessary for the success of any business."

It works. It really does. The only problem is that it burns people out. Managers must manage during the day and plan at night (or do neither very well). They may be spending tremendous time on bringing in lower costs or higher quality. When this burns out the best managers, their own absence isn't part of the plan. Long-range planning may work to the company's disadvantage if it destroys vital individuals in a company—without planning how to gain new talent. Here's the contradiction. If those managers saw that their own burn-out and replacement were planned in (as a good, detailed plan would show), they would get out sooner, trading off a high salary against quality of life and, possibly, length of life.

Businesses that do little detailed planning are also successful. Yet conventional wisdom has it that detailed, long-range planning is necessary, so we devote thousands of unproductive hours to meticulous planning and replanning, perhaps only to give an *appearance* of planning. It is possible, of course, that planning is the last step in the evolution of a totally uninvolved, "spectator" mentality which begins with T.V. and continues into the work place in the form of elaborate planning, monitoring, evaluating, and replanning.

3. "It's much better to buy a new car than to inherit someone else's problems."

The new car syndrome is based on the fixed trade-off this conventional wisdom bestows on the buying public. When we buy a new car, are we not also paying for: (1) society's concern for energy and pollution and (2) automakers' problems with increased material costs, increased wages, and declining productivity? Even common sense could tell us that a car with 40,000 miles on it has "proven it isn't a lemon." But common sense is very different from conventional wisdom.

Let's make a bottom-line analysis of this "new car." I can buy a good used car for $1,500 or a new car for $7,500 ($1,500 down, $6,000 on a forty-eight-month plan). The $1,500 used car investment won't depreciate as much, and I could buy four more used cars at that price over an eight-year period, if I needed to. If I got back *half* that money on each one, I'd end up with $3,750. When the $7,500 car is eight years old, it would be worth $1,500. After eight years I would have lost $6,000 on the *new* car, while I would still have at least $3,750 from my used cars to buy another used car. Worst possibility: Even if repairs cost me half that (and they usually wouldn't unless all four cars were lemons), I'd still have $1,875 to buy that eight-year-old "new car." I would have saved $1,500 interest. Best possibility: I'd have no repairs, drive the first car eight years, and save $6,000.

TIP 2. Conventional Wisdom Usually Creates a Large Worth Context.

A lot of people will spend a lot of money over a long period of time to support their conventional wisdom. If you are looking for a worth context which is lasting, consider the lines of thought that lead from conventional wisdom. In other words, you can get out of the trap of believing this wisdom is "fixed" and into trade-off opportunities in the same shift of thought. You could, for example:

1. Predict the "understood employee" conventional wisdom to last five more years, until we've got to do something productive toavoid national bankruptcy. By that time you can have made enough money consulting with managers on the subject to buy stock, land, or an entire business at rock-bottom prices.
2. Predict the future attrition rate of long-range planning managers to be high, and start an executive search firm for middle managers to take up the long-range planning torch when present managers burn themselves out.
3. Predict that the "new car" syndrome will last ten more years but that poor assembly to hold down prices will result in needing more repairs. Invest in an auto repair business to accommodate expected breakdowns.

Conventional wisdom creates illusory trade-offs that remain "fixed" and "real" only as long as we consider them "fixed" and "real." But the minute we see a precept of conventional wisdom as wrong, or as only one point of view, we begin to see trade-off opportunities abounding, practically creating themselves.

Good traders look at their "fixed" trade-offs with some skepticism, not only to recognize trade-off "traps" and to see what is fixed and what is not, but to seek hidden opportunities which may result from "unfixing" those trade-offs. The perspectives a good trader takes always vary with the situation. Sometimes we reexamine what we had considered a "fixed" trade-off *because* we have a strong opportunity. And other times, shedding a "fixed" trade-off perception *makes* the opportunity.

To be free from conventional wisdom as a "fixed" trade-off is perhaps the greatest advantage a trader can have. When traders unwittingly share the mass belief that things "must" remain (or progress) in a certain way, they cut themselves off from a large sector of possibilities on the trading ground. That is why the most successful traders become dedicated students of:

What Iffing

Twixtward Eight

The trade-off traps of *structures, commitments, habits,* and *conventional wisdom* are never fixed.

Structures can be escaped by innovation or reinterpretation.

Commitments can be modified or waited out.

Habits can be changed or broken.

Conventional Wisdom is often partly or wholly wrong—especially by the time millions accept it, any truth it had may have been lost in the shift of events. Like the extracted wisdom tooth, we may wonder why we ever thought we needed it.

The main thing is to know these "traps" are not fixed unless you *make* them fixed. The first step toward any opportunity, then, is to realize the trap is the result of a negotiated settlement with yourself. And negotiations are always renegotiable.

The second step is to ask:

What If?

9

Trade-Off Opportunities

Opportunity may knock only once but we knock opportunities constantly.

Artists, children, and inventors who sit daydreaming have all been accused of "what iffing." But not managers. Not traders. Not responsible people like we are supposed to be . . . Not us.

But there is a corner of the trading ground populated by the most prosperous among us, and we wonder how they, the mysteriously successful, evolved out of our own kind. There is, of course, an answer: they have learned how to play "what if."

Perhaps they learned it from artists and inventors. Or even a child pulling up the daisies. At any rate, they have surely learned it, for we hear them say:

>*"What if* the value of the dollar falls?"
>*"What if* they pass the business tax credit?"
>*"What if* our present chemical vendor runs short?"

What we hear is a stream of "what ifs" that eventually leads to better trade-offs. Much of the business of business concerns projecting future trade-offs or trading off the least possible now to achieve the best trade-off situation in the future. When we project future trade-offs, of course, we always aim at higher quality for lower cost and lower time. To do that, a trader must become very good at "what iffing":

>*"What if* our competition gets to the market ahead of us?"
>*"What if* the government requires an immediate vested retirement plan?"
>*"What if* we must change to other energy sources?"

In each case, the answer *cannot* be "que será, será." Imagine seriously telling your business partner:

>"Well . . . if this business fails we can always start another. Or maybe live off unemployment benefits for a while."

Not only business, but every forward-looking family, every wise person, builds contingencies into their present trade-offs. So, for example, when wondering,

>*"What if* our present chemical vendor runs short?"

the wise manager thinks:

>"I might have to pay more for smaller orders in a short time from three vendors, but I will be covered in case one runs short."

When the businesswoman's current trade-off is this . . .

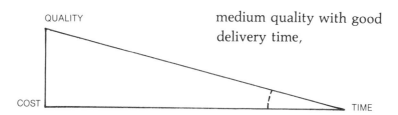

medium quality with good delivery time,

she envisions that it might become this,

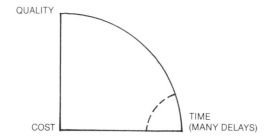

so she modifies her current trade-off to this.

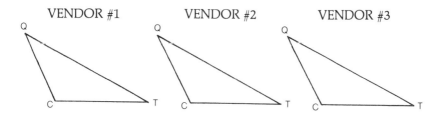

In the process, she may also come up with something she never expected . . . Higher quality because she is buying in smaller lots, but demonstrating the potential to buy larger volume from any one supplier. She has inadvertently run into a "eureka," a contingency trade-off that has another desired effect she had not even suspected. Then, if she carries this notion of competition out, she will realize that this gives her a chance to constantly compare prices, service, and product reliability of each vendor against the other two. This is a more frequent occurrence than you might suspect: by "what iffing" and making a minor adjustment to a present trade-off, another benefit can be achieved unexpectedly.

"What iffing" usually falls into three broad categories. *What if:*

We stop doing something we are doing?
We do something new?
We change the way we are doing this?

Some might say that "what iffing" is somewhere between daydreaming and worrying, but either way, there are several opportunities for new trade-offs which can be seen from playing "what if."

Abandonment—What If We Stop?

Abandonment begins with the question, "What if we stop doing _____ (what we are doing)?" The question allows us to isolate that activity from the rest of the world and to see how our other trade-offs might be without it. Often that vision raises another question, "Can we afford *not* to stop doing _____ ?"

Sometimes it takes personal courage, and sometimes just brisk business logic. A layoff at a company is often due to abandoning some product. But then some companies go bankrupt rather than lay anyone off. History is replete with examples of staunchly maintaining the status quo even though doing so resulted in dire, dismal consequences.

We've spent years trading off the world's oil reserves to clad ourselves in tons of metal. Did we learn abandonment too late?

In the nineteenth century Americans carried extra pounds on their bodies, under the supposition that "fat showed prosperity." More recently we realize that early death is often caused by this extra load.

Abandonment means not only streamlining a body or a business. It means *divesting* one weight, so that you can carry another or move more freely. Either way the tough choice of abandonment is often necessary before you have the freedom to make other choices. Abandonment may be crucial to making any of the right moves at all. The time and effort spent in preserving what should be abandoned may do worse than starve your best potential; it may encourage you to invest time and money in failing enterprises.

Let's say you have three parts to your business: wire making, metal cladding, and a cosmetics line acquired by your predecessor in an attempt to diversify.

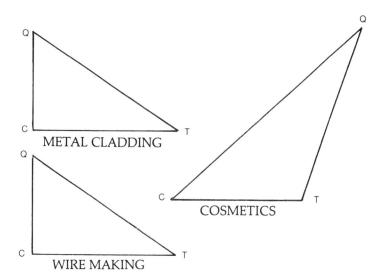

METAL CLADDING

COSMETICS

WIRE MAKING

Even though the cosmetics branch could make money, it is so different from the other two operations that you cannot set company-wide practices because the cosmetics operation has totally different demands. The extra operation, even though it might be self-sustaining, causes an immense time drain on you and the company, taking away from planning and strategies that could increase quality in metal cladding and wire making.

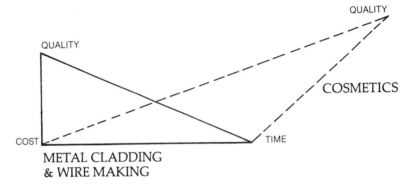

METAL CLADDING
& WIRE MAKING

If you abandon the cosmetics operation, the remaining business could look like this.

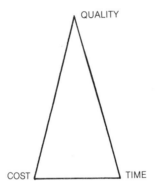

And perhaps eventually like this.

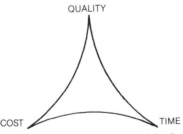

But the cosmetics business would have to become astronomically profitable to justify the time you invest in dealing with this distinctly different operation. Abandonment of it, on the other hand, could give you both the time and working capital to make the other two businesses more successful.

Whenever abandonment is used positively, it is so that remaining resources can be used in the worth context while they are still valuable. The worth context comes and goes; so it is crucial to abandon whatever needs abandoning *in time.*

> The small aircraft flying on one engine must dump excess baggage and fuel *before* it hits the mountain, so that it can gain altitude to reach the airfield on the other side.

> The product whose competition already sells at half the price must be abandoned before it goes on the market.

> The engineering student who flunks all elective philosophy courses better abandon that interest before he sacrifices his grade point.

Why do we continue doing things that give us unfortunate trade-off positions? Perhaps we are trading off dreams of quality, allegiance to a once good product ("if only we could build the luxury car market back up"), allegiance to people ("Martha was once the most promising manager here"), past glory ("if only we could pull together that team we had in the old days"), past romance ("maybe it could be like it was").

Hope is the foundation of trade-off opportunities. But hope is much better directed toward the wild possibilities of the future than re-creation of a successful past. And abandonment is the unshackling of that hope from the trade-offs of the past.

Risking—What If We Try Something New?

Another "what iffing" question asked more often than "What if we stop _____ ?" is "What if we do something we haven't been doing?" Then we can ask, "What if we do and something happens we didn't expect?" But we can also ask, "What if we don't and wish we had?"

All this "what iffing" concerns risk.

Risk is the speculative trade-off that carries some probability for future gain in improving cost, quality, or time. Few prizes of any consequence were won without it. Books are written on games that involve risk, and there is no poker guide or manual on beating the odds in Las Vegas that will say you can play these games *without* risk. So the question is not *whether* to risk but—if we wish to stay in the game—*how much to risk and when.*

Risks are taken in order to (1) get you somewhere you're not or (2) keep you somewhere you are but won't be for long if you sit still. If we are looking at life games, we must also consider the risk of *not* risking, of not going all out when the worth context is right. If you look at your own value and its growth, you may want to look at the probabilities not only of your advancing (winning) but of slipping backward. When the season of a worth context declines, your worth may fall also. You may want to say, "If I take the risk, it has a 70 percent probability of success, and if I don't it has a 70 percent chance of falling below the status quo." But if one considered the increments of upward and downward possibilities, it might look like this.

Risk Probabilities

NO RISK (DON'T)		RISK (DO)
	Great success	20%
10%	Some growth	50%
20%	Status quo	10%
20%	Slow decline	10%
50%	Rapid failure	10%

Yes, it would be a black day if you lost everything. But real opportunity inevitably requires taking some incremental risk, at least when:

> The chances of success are high.
> Some reasonable portion of the losses can be recouped.

Most companies want managers who "know how to take risks." That means they want the managers to:

1. Be able to "what if" in order to identify areas of opportunity.
2. Know what can be risked.
3. Know the odds on the potential payoff.
4. Plan contingency moves for recouping possible losses.

A modern "risking tool" business has refined for its own use is forecasting. It may be easy to plot trends for price increases and labor costs, but in sales forecasting one would expect the crystal ball to be hazy. By using a hazy crystal ball rather than none, salespeople are able to rate prospects, predict orders, and set priorities for the best results. That's what forecasting should be: a tool for risking—for placing your best resources and efforts in the places where the probabilities are highest.

Risking is, of course, an attempt to jump from one trade-off to another. For example, the company that puts 1 percent of its earnings into research and development risks that amount hoping it will get . . .

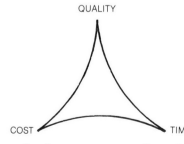

a quality product in little time at a small investment . . .

out of at least one research project and betting that at least all of those efforts won't turn out . . .

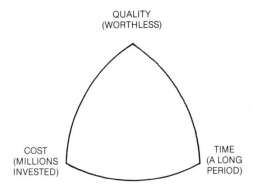

If the 1 percent it put in someday generates 10 percent more earnings than there might have been, the investment paid off. If not, that 1 percent was a gesture, a tip of the hat to progress.

Now let's look at the fine points of risks, because most of the risks we take in management are concerned with improving quality *slightly,* cutting time *slightly,* or cutting costs *slightly.*

We may have to risk cutting quality *slightly* to cut costs.

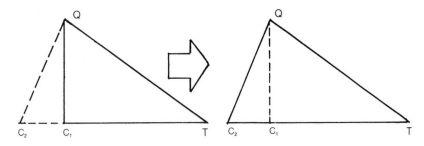

Or to get something done on a tighter schedule, we may have to raise costs (e.g., pay for overtime labor).

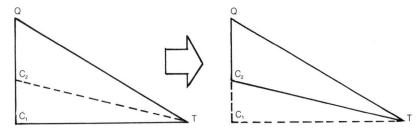

In each of these cases, there is a *risk* that competitors will come up with an opposite trade-off. For instance, you cut cost by cutting quality while

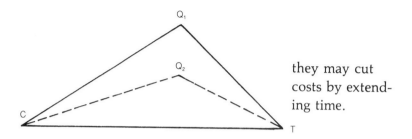

they may cut costs by extend-ing time.

"Takes two weeks longer but it's highly reliable."

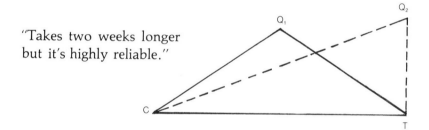

If the market cares more about quality (say, for watches) than it does about *time* (say, for back-to-school supplies or Halloween trinkets), and you traded off quality to cut costs on watches, you risked the wrong thing. If you cut quality to cut costs but got Halloween goods to the store on time, you risked correctly.

Most important of all:

If you kept your trade-offs fixed, you didn't make much money.

The operation that is too expensive, even if it's there on time with the quality, is eating itself up internally. This is just one example of risks that are *necessary* to business and where fixed trade-offs are detrimental.

Learning Curves—What If We Change the Way We Do It?

There are numerous situations which cause us to *react* with changes in the way we do things: expanding costs, competition, improved technology, and so on. We react to improve our efficiency or cost effectiveness. One objective of "what iffing" is to take advance action on costs, competition, and technology which has not yet come to pass (but probably will). This combination of "what iffing" and taking action in advance is made possible by our past experience, both as individuals and as whole businesses. If we can look *back* on what we have learned, we can also look forward to what we *will* learn in the future. By expecting that we will learn, we can forecast and design toward the unknown. Banking on the fact that we will learn by doing, we can act upon the future and open trade-off opportunities we might not have suspected. But, let's start at the beginning.

Perhaps the greatest trade-off opportunity of all is learning, for when you trade a few dollars and a few hours to learn something, it seems to magnify your possibilities. And it offers a way to approach the best of all trade-offs: low cost, high quality, and low time.

In most situations where a worker is learning a skill, the supervisor can usually see what is known as a "learning curve." As the worker tries to do the job, the efforts are at first halting. After a few days, efforts are slow but smooth, and with that comes a measurable increase in units the new worker can produce in a day.

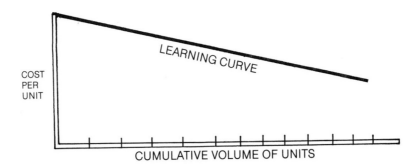

This phenomenon called the "learning curve" seems to *just happen* anytime there is volume demand combined with limited time and labor so that the process doesn't slacken. In the midst of such scurry, the sole requirement for the learning curve to take effect for individual workers—or a whole operation—is that they don't give up. They continue what they are doing and keep trying to do it better and faster and cheaper.

And in that melee something happens. The assembler discovers a simpler way to lay out parts and eureka! Speed is doubled. This allows the supervisor to use one less worker and put one more inspector on the line and eureka! Better yield with fewer rejects. The productivity of the whole operation just doubled! What happened? Creativity. Innovation. Learning . . . perhaps magic.

It is magic. But in the engineering world (where they must quantify even magic) it is known as a "step function."

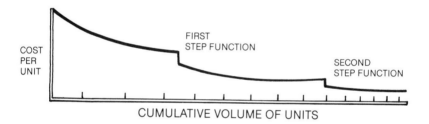

CUMULATIVE VOLUME OF UNITS

The term *step function* sounds bland, calculated, but it raises engineers and manufacturers to bristling excitement whenever they hear it because it involves *human* conquest in the midst of numbers and hard physical realities. It is the eureka of creativity read in the dryness of a manufacturing report. What happens, in the case of almost every such learning experience, is the same. A plateau is reached, we continue at the same level, then eureka! In an instant, all becomes clear and we move to the next plateau of better understanding and performance as if by a quantum leap.

It has happened to all of us.

And it happens to whole operations—even whole businesses—if conditions are right, *if* there is enough volume to create a pattern of experience, *and if* the step function is valued.

More important . . . it is possible to *design* the process. The business person who thinks this way

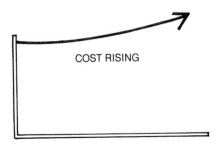

will probably *have* higher costs, a self-fulfilling prophecy. But the person who thinks this way

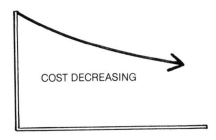

will probably, by the same self-fulfilling prophecy, experience a "learning curve."

The point here is that by observing the learning curve we can sometimes see what it will *take* to bring the curve down a "step." If we can't see what it will take, we will be able to position ourselves as advantageously on the curve as possible and be ready for the eureka which takes us the next step to even better performance. In some industries, conscious planning for step functions—which occur predictably although their nature cannot be foretold—is known as "design-to-cost."

Design-to-Cost

Design-to-cost is a planning process *committed* to the innovation that *invariably* accompanies experience. Design-to-cost is a result of learning about learning and is based on the value of that experience in finding creative solutions. It takes the experience of several learning curves and uses these as the foundation for *early* trade-offs, based on faith that those learning curve principles will also be working in new circumstances, as the new learning experience unfolds.

Design-to-cost involves betting on a reasonable future rather than shying away from making trade-offs now that could make more things possible in the future. It is a philosophy based on expectations and on self-fulfilling prophecies.

The name *design-to-cost* comes from the business practice of entering the market at one price and bringing production costs down to a much lower price by a specific future date.

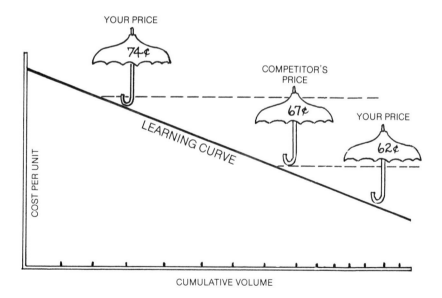

For instance, if you introduce a product in the market at 74 cents and continue selling at that price, you will create a price "umbrella" under which any competitor can slip with a comparable product for 67 cents. Then you drop your price to 62 cents, and if you don't go broke, you will be hurting financially before one of you is shaken out of the market.

However, if you had *aimed* at reducing cost at planned intervals, you could plan how much of a share of the market you'd get and how much volume you could produce. Of course, that's where you must have faith in how much you will learn in the future. You've designed for step functions you cannot define, but which you *know* will occur in using materials, developing better methods, or reducing overhead along the way. You know it will happen because it always does, if the production volume and specific expectations are present.

There are some usual things you can predict happening with a learning curve, when it applies to an operation with such volume and designed expectations.

1. The time to complete a process will drop dramatically at first, then more gradually, until it reaches a plateau.

2. If volume and expectations do *not* diminish, there will usually appear one or more possible step functions which make increased performance (less time or cost for the same or better quality) possible.

3. The step function entails more cost or time for a short while, and it may become a trade-off where volume justifies a step function (such as new and better equipment).

4. In many cases, the step function does not involve cost or time, but merely reorganization of the process. The recognition of *how* the process can be better organized is the result of learning.

5. Some step functions must follow one another, and some may occur at random with beneficial effect. New materials, for example, may have to wait for the purchase of new equipment. But *shared experience*—from, say, one assembler to another—can dramatically improve the results of an operation at any time.

What designing-to-cost allows, then, is a series of trade-offs built on future expectations. The person who wants to have the best trade-off six months from now envisions his activity *now* and builds his trade-offs for now on his faith that the process he is involved in *will* become less time-consuming, and that useful step functions *will* occur, even if he cannot yet envision them.

Whole businesses, in fact, may use this philosophy to enter the market with a low price despite high start-up costs, knowing that down the learning curve their costs and time will drop to accommodate the volume of buyers attracted by lower prices. The most dynamic example of this has been in the semiconductor industry.

The semiconductor industry freed electronics from the vacuum tube. No longer were electronic products prohibitive in size, as miniature electronic components for transistor radios, computers, watches, and pocket calculators enabled manufacturers to fill consumer needs in a way previously thought impossible.

In the cut-throat competition which ensued, *manufacturing innovation* was the key, and innovation took place (and still does) so rapidly that the first hand-held calculators which sold for $169 *had* to sell for $19.95 two years later to stay in competition. Here's why: Company X could enter the market and hold profits after a certain reduction, creating a price umbrella.

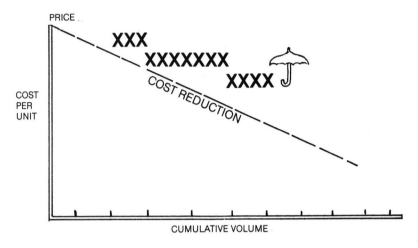

Then company Y could come along, running *closer* in price to the learning curve in the industry, until it levelled off and created a similar umbrella.

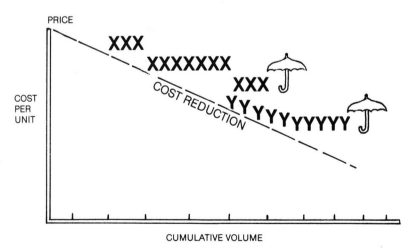

And then company Z could slip in under company Y's umbrella by running even closer to the learning curve.

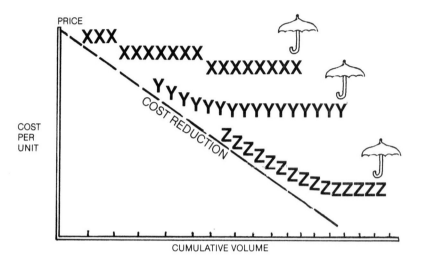

So it soon became apparent that the price of goods in that market had to follow a close margin above the production cost reductions that occurred because of the learning curve. Large profits could only be made if a large enough share of the market were captured by lower prices to allow the learning curve to take effect with its step-function improvement due to volume demands.

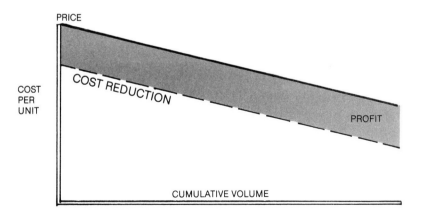

The semiconductor industry's problem is to keep enough innovation in manufacturing methods to win what has become a "race down the learning curve." But the runner with the head start doesn't always win. Two things affect winning or losing this "race."

MARKET SHARE

If a company keeps prices up to make a profit, it loses its market share. If it loses market share, its sales orders do not produce enough volume demands for the learning curve to take effect.

LEADING EDGE TECHNOLOGY

Obviously, the company first into the market (with the necessary quality) has, for a short while, the *whole* market. However, if it does not generate enough volume in sales by using that advantage, someone else's newer technology will grab the leading edge and capture part or all of the market share.

A further finding about the learning curve in the semiconductor market is that it becomes steeper with more volume, because more volume means more experience in making the product and hence the potential for more step-function innovations. So, more step functions experienced more rapidly yield more and more rapid cost reductions. These make the slope steep and the "race" faster for those who can keep up.

The process of innovation must be *planned* and *continuous* in this industry, and the pace is breathtaking. Design-to-cost, then, is its *proactive* method of planning that "race" down the learning curve far ahead of actually entering the market. In many cases, a thorough design-to-cost effort precedes a company's decision to enter the market. That decision is based on what amount of market share can be expected to produce what step-function innovations. Creativity becomes a planned and expected phenomenon in electronics, to the benefit of everyone except those who can't keep the pace.

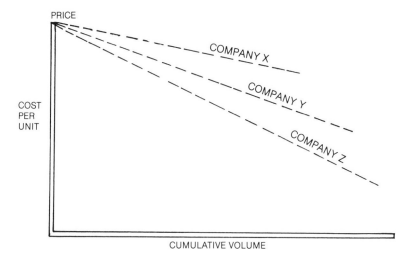

Managers in most businesses could take advantage of this kind of thinking, however, because learning curve phenomena are not limited to electronics or manufacturing. You can determine the correctness of its premise from experience, and you can bet on yourself in the future. That's what designing-to-cost is: being committed to a reasonable future of learning and creativity rather than shying away from the trade-offs that make those opportunities possible.

In looking at this most attractive trade-off opportunity, remember that to take advantage of the learning curve you must:

1. Know that the activity will be repeated.
2. Believe, based on past experience, that time for the activity will decrease.
3. Design in any step functions you know about beforehand.
4. Have faith that step functions will occur.
5. Commit yourself to being there. No excuses.

Do not wander down plateau after plateau in any process you (or your operation) is involved in. Judging from experience, set slopes for improvement based on expectations that the learning curve *will* happen and that step functions will occur.

In the end, you may achieve a super trade-off, with high quality at low cost and low time. But such situations only come about through faith and planning. The step function is not totally predictable—or even rational—and so the planning process which designs in step functions is truly a wager on human innovation.

Twixtward Nine

"What iffing" may lead us into:

Abandonment—"What if we stop doing what we are doing?"
Risking—"What if we try something new?"
Learning Curves—"What if we change the way we are doing this?"

Abandonment can free trade-off possibilities. *Risking* may be the only way to increase results, and *learning curves* may offer us "step functions" on the way toward new plateaus of achievement. *Designing-to-cost* is a bet on the self-fulfilling prophecy of the learning curve. It shows, time and again, that a goal commitment brings unexpected creativity and ingenuity in its attainment.

The chapters up to now have all been concerned with your individual perceptions of trade-offs. Most of them apply equally to actions in business or private life, but all have been explained in terms of things that affect you and the trade-offs you make to find a better situation.

But if you are a manager, of any kind, there are other people in your galaxy, and they too are traders. How you trade off affects how they trade off, always.

10

Planets in Your System

Without his two turtles supporting him, Atlas would have plunged through outer space.

There are systems larger than you and systems that are smaller and depend on you. If you lead or supervise others in any way, then your trades are their trades, too. You will find that supporting your own system is crucial to your trades within the galaxies and with the stars that orbit in constant possibilities.

Remember that every person in your system is also a trader, and every person there is constantly making trades and, at the same time, worrying about your trading them off.

In some companies employees work better if they feel they are part of a "family." They are not quite so concerned about impact areas (though the ambitious always are). Companies that treat those employees as "family" pride themselves in having few layoffs and few firings. They just transfer people and give them other jobs in the "family." In one such company, coffee was free during coffee breaks in every plant of the company of 70,000. This resulted in camaraderie and a closely knit culture from which management benefited immensely, since there was low turnover and a merely average pay scale could attract and keep employees.

Then one financial manager, eager to reduce cost, pointed out that free coffee cost the company $300,000 a year. Top management approved the demise of free coffee. What happened?

The family broke up. Soon the company lost valuable people in turnover and had to pay more for the ones who stayed. For something as prosaic as free coffee, employees felt they had been traded off once and probably would be again. So they began to individualize their trade-offs, and that meant dissolution of the "family."

This is not a common example, of course. Most businesses have been forced to abandon "family" concepts, and the results of the limited trade-offs available to managers can be read in union demands, EEO class action suits, and the high cost of every kind of labor.

Britain shows us another example, by the way. Whenever British unions strike, the only thing management *can* offer workers is more money. It has been speculated that if management were able to provide status and dignity to the working person, there would not be as great a cry for money. Then inflation would not push Britain to the edge of bankruptcy. One might say that British management refuses (or knows not how) to trade what the working person *really* wants.

If you manage others, be sure you know what they really want. It may not be money alone. It may be more dignity, more responsibility, more worth. Very likely what they will want is *leadership*, providing direction for their best efforts.

Some old but good maxims for leadership are:

"You can't fool the troops."

"Stand up for your people."

"In that ye do it unto the least of them, ye do it unto me."

"If people in a company aren't performing well, don't get new people, get a new president."

Another maxim might be:

"If you trade off employees, they'll trade you off."

Subordinates have more power to influence our performance than we sometimes remember. If we:

Work them long and hard with no rewards—they'll leave, slow down, or begin making costly blunders.

Aggrandize ourselves for work they've done—they'll do much less work.

Tell them how to do something they are quite capable of doing—they will allow us to take up our time and energy telling them, and then following our orders, botch it.

Confuse them with our indecision—their work will be erratic.

Ask that they be punctual when we are not—they won't understand, at all . . .

That is why performance appraisals are so difficult to administer well, because if we are honest, we know that our employees' performance reflects our leadership in so many ways:

In the resources we've put at their disposal
In the example we've set
In the freedom we've given them to do their best work
(rather than requesting too many reports and looking
over their shoulders)
In the amount of information we've given them about
why they are doing something
In the amount of thoughtful feedback we've given
which has enabled them to adjust their course
In the ways we've sought to develop their abilities

Because we must weigh *these* things carefully when we review their performance, we are reviewing ourselves. That's why it's difficult. That's why so many poor managers stall when giving formal reviews or avoid them completely.

Look at it this way . . . when you conduct performance reviews, employees are merely asking that you trade with them the way you would trade with your peers or supervisors. If you are in the position of managing several people, try these avenues of sharing trade-offs which affect them.

1. DISCLOSE AND SHARE RESULTS WITH THEM.
   Profit sharing is an obvious positive sharing, but sometimes disclosure about a negative trade-off can have the positive result of building employees' trust in your leadership. More than one major company has made a policy of telling employees when there is going to be a layoff and *who* is most likely to be laid off and even offers outplacement for employees who've been "traded off." In some cases, companies will institute unpaid holidays between Christmas and New Year up to the highest level of management, to share the problem of low paychecks equally.

2. CONSULT THEM ABOUT THE SITUATION.
   "We can go X route or Y route and end up at the same place. What's your preference?"

3. OFFER SPECIFIC EXPECTATIONS FOR THEM TO WORK
TOWARD.

Perhaps this above all is the key to getting better performance and happier workers. If you merely have the power
of your position and can't explain what performance you
want specifically, then you are riding a wild elephant, and
no wonder employees scurry out of your sight. But real
power, the power of forming and communicating specific
expectations, can draw out an employee's best efforts,
growth, and ingenuity. Without your even asking. And
that is leadership at its best.

There are also aching trade-offs, the ones that feel forced
upon you, or worse, the ones brought about by your inability
to see a way out:

When you have to transfer or fire someone
When you have to reject an idea someone has worked
on a lot
When you have to choose between two deserving
people for promotion.

If you look at them as present or potential trade-offs, the
path can become at least a little better thought out.

1. If you have to pay a person for no work or spend an inor-
dinate amount of time to get the lowest level in quality,
your trade-off is

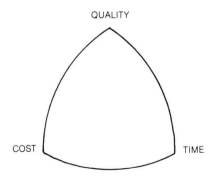

(the worst).

The new person you hire will either cost (for competence)

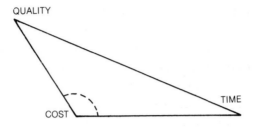

or take time to train.

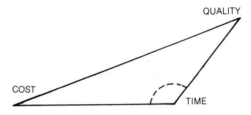

(This lost time during the worth context may cost, too.)

Either way, you have a much better set of trade-offs to work with if you replace the consistently poor performer.

2. Try analyzing (and disclosing your analysis of) any employee's ideas you reject by explaining that he or she trades off too much of one thing to achieve another. The marketing person who wants to get in far ahead of the competition by sacrificing cost and quality should understand (if not accept) your priorities.

3. To keep your choice between two deserving people for promotion as objective as possible, you might judge their performance and potential against the trade-off triangles. Candidate A may have a high appreciation for quality and cost but very little for time.

Candidate A

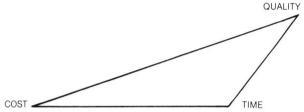

Candidate B may have a good ability to cut cost and time but without proper emphasis on quality.

Candidate B

Your perception of what the position needs, in terms of a trade-off inclination, can provide one factor that you might use in your final selection.

Trade-off inclination may also be a very important factor when you are selected to manage. That is because your higher managers are not only looking at your education, experience, and demonstrated competence. They are also deciding whether they want to put balance or lean into this prospective operation.

Balance and Lean

As a manager you have to make a number of trades which have *balance* foremost in mind, and some which exaggerate one or another trade-off. The manager of an operation which by nature distinctly *leans* toward cost, quality, or time is constantly caught between preserving the balance that gives the operation stability and exaggerating the trade-off *lean* that seems to offer the most promise. In a given situation, there are advantages to both balance and lean. Yet you can't have both at once.

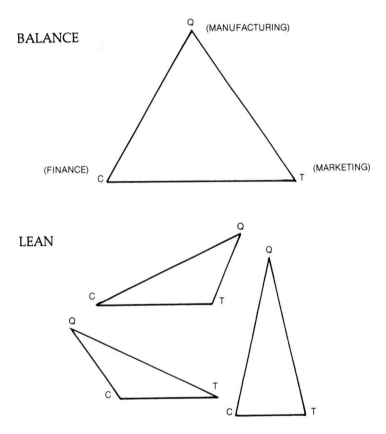

BALANCE

Q (MANUFACTURING)

(FINANCE) C

T (MARKETING)

LEAN

In an earlier example of marketing (time) versus finance (cost) versus manufacturing (quality) inclinations, the company manager would have the very real concern of keeping balance or *equilibrium* in the trade-off set. The advantages in doing so would be:

1. REPUTATION OF FAIR DEALING WITH EMPLOYEES.
   Even if the marketing people wanted the product *now*, they would be almost as competitive a month from now.

The manufacturing people could do fine with a quality control standard of 94 percent rather than 97 percent, and the finance people should be happy enough with a 25 percent return on investment as opposed to their desired 30 percent. So one advantage of trading off with balance in mind is "fairness." In the long run, this can be an investment in keeping employees, predictable performance, and so on.

2. FALL BACK POSITIONS.

If the manager traded off to maintain equilibrium, he or she probably made sure there was "fall back" strength in each area. The finance people feeling fairly dealt with at 25 percent return on investment (as they might not have at 10 percent) will at times provide the grace for you to "fall back" to 17 percent or 18 percent to allow expansion, overtime, or new equipment purchases. At the same time, if manufacturing has worked under fair quality standards, it may occasionally fall back to two inspectors per line rather than three. And marketing, having been given fair speed to market on one product, may relent on that speed for some products that do not depend so much on rapid release to compete.

There are also disadvantages to the equilibrium approach.

1. EQUILIBRIUM BECOMES ALL IMPORTANT.

In his recent book *Systemantics,* John Gall postulates that any system established to do a job immediately develops internal objectives which are more important to the system than the job it was created to do.

EXAMPLE: A system which promotes on *seniority alone,* for example, is trying to maintain internal equilibrium, regardless of the consequences to the product that operation is supposed to provide. When there are people who could do the job better and they are *not* promoted, then that treasured equilibrium is destructive.

2. OPPORTUNITIES USUALLY HAVE A DISTINCT TRADE-OFF
"LEAN."

Any opportunity of consequence usually has a substantial
"lean" toward one type of trade-off or another.

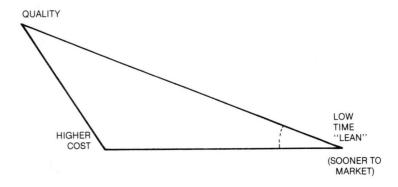

EXAMPLE: A product for the summer will sell like mad if
you have it in distributors' hands by March. After that
you've lost the fox. Therefore, a manager who doesn't
"lean with" the low time trade-off is not getting the job
done.

EXAMPLE: If low cost of the product is the highest priority, then the manager who allows marketing to spend a lot
promoting it, or lets manufacturing spend the money on
materials to make its quality exceptional, is allowing
balance in the operation to outweigh opportunities.

EXAMPLE: Finally, if the quality of the product is the
prime concern in a sale, as in the diamond market, then
customers usually have to wait *and* pay for that quality.

Any sprinter will tell you, you can't run straight up. To get
your body moving, you have to lean severely *out of balance*, in
the direction of the race. On the other hand, any distance runner will tell you that the economy and efficiency of the body can
only be maintained for the distance if you don't lean too far forward.

This is an analogy of the manager's dilemma. One set of trade-offs offers stability and peace of mind. The other is crucial to achieving. If you nod in agreement that you too share this dilemma, remember those who run your galaxy also must constantly decide between "balance" and "lean."

Twixtward Ten

We work for traders, we work with traders, and we have traders working for us. When traders work for us, we must be conscious of how our trade-offs affect their trade-offs.

As managers of traders, we vary between stabilizing the activity by a *balance* of trade-offs, giving equal import to cost, quality, and time.

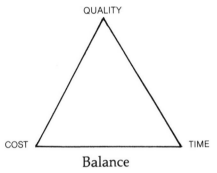

Balance

But at times we must give the activity impetus by making it *lean* toward one trade-off or another. One example would be in the rush of getting a seasonal product to market, when time is of the highest priority and cost and quality must be traded off.

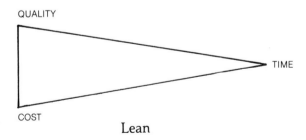

Lean

So the manager is almost always pulled—between maintaining equilibrium and fairness by *balancing* trade-offs and seizing new opportunities by *leaning* them toward crucial priorities.

11

Pulling Up Stakes

When you first came to the trading ground, you may or may not have had suitable tools or a good map. You may have had trading experiences like some we've seen here, or you may be eager now to try them. If you take these few things with you, you will have gained the best of bargains.

1. Cost, quality, and time are at stake in every trading situation.
2. Trade-offs begin with trading with yourself.
3. Your trade-off inclination tells you which trade-off is better than another.
4. Knowing other people's trade-off inclinations helps resolve conflicts.
5. Seeing larger galaxies of trade-offs and recognizing impact areas helps you avoid being traded off.

6. Getting out of trade-off traps helps you grasp opportunities.
7. Asking "what if" opens new trade-off opportunities for you.
8. Believing in the learning curve and designing-to-cost for the future provides the greatest opportunities of all.
9. When managing people, you manage other traders and will always have to consider whether you're striking for balance or lean in your trade-offs.

Thanks

To Leslie Stephen, who demonstrates that an editor may be as important to a book as its writer;

to Ray Bard, the astute publisher;

to Larry Davis, the astute;

to the Learning Concepts staff for their forebearance and care;

and

to all the people who reviewed earlier drafts and helped the book finally survive.

About the Author

National Training Manager of the American Heart Association, David Hon is also a prolific writer. In addition to *Trade-Offs* he has written another book, *Meetings That Matter*, a number of articles for national trade journals, numerous instructional videotapes and films, and an award winning play. He is also a member of the editorial board for *Training Magazine*.

Prior to his work with the American Heart Association, David was a program manager for Texas Instruments where he developed worldwide training programs in management, sales and personnel.

A graduate of the University of Washington and the University of Tulsa, David holds a masters degree in communications.

He is currently developing and patenting a computer/videodisc training system.

David, like all of us, has made thousands of trade-offs and expects to be making many more. His current trading ground is Dallas, Texas.